THE DAY
I BECAME
THE SPIDER KILLER

— CHRISTINE MALONE —

A MEMOIR OF
TRAUMA, TRAGEDY AND SURVIVAL

"Christine's account will touch you. Hers is a story of great pain and desperation, but of greater resilience. She is a survivor."

- Sara H.

"Christine's writing evokes mixed feelings of sadness, yet warm fuzzies in me."

- Cheryl M.

"Christine has lived a life well-lived...her beautifully written book takes you through a life that includes tragic loss, but also includes great triumphs, despite the losses. A journey that reveals how to fight and endure, even when it seems that the world-and particularly the healthcare system-may be working against you. Reading this colorful life story brings hope, and helps others feel that they are not alone in darkness that may impact their lives."

- Mario F.

The Day I Became the Spider Killer:

A Memoir of Trauma, Tragedy, and Survival

By

Christine Malone

Life is not meant to be a smooth path. It is the bumps along the way that make us the individuals we are – each episode causing a twist, a turn, as well as physical and emotional scars. For some, those bumps happen more often than for others. I've heard it said that life is not about what happens to you but about how you handle the things you go through. There is no one way to react to trauma or tragedy, there is only the way that works best for each one of us individually.

"When disaster causes the familiar ground to shudder beneath the feet of a child, a neurotic is sometimes born, or a writer, and often both." Quote from Time magazine (May 20, 1957)

Chapter 1:

Early Childhood in a Dysfunctional Home

"Abuse manipulates and twists a child's natural sense of trust and love. Her innocent feelings are belittled or mocked, and she learns to ignore her feelings. She can't afford to feel the full range of feelings in her body while she's being abused—pain, outrage, hate, vengeance, confusion, arousal. So, she short-circuits them and goes numb. For many children, any expression of feelings, even a single tear, is cause for more severe abuse. Again, the only recourse is to shut down. Feelings go underground."

— *Laura Davis*

Invisibility. As far back as I can remember, that was the superpower I longed for. To be invisible was to be safe. This started in early childhood and continued into adulthood - a desire to be unseen. Being seen was negative on so many levels. One of my earliest childhood memories is one where I am hiding in a closet. I can see the light between the two closet doors, and I know my mother is looking for me. The closet was full of my mother's clothes and the smell of her perfume. As she walked by, with her hairbrush in her hand, she said, "You know I will find you!" She held that hairbrush in her right hand, smacking it against the palm of her left hand. My three-year-old mind weighed my options – I could remain hidden, which would only increase her anger, and I knew I would eventually be found. Or I could show myself and hope that my mother's anger, and subsequent punishment, would be less. Though this memory, including the sounds and smells, is very vivid, I do not remember the choice I made. I don't remember being found, though I know (of course) that I was.

My parents married in July 1962. My sister, Lori, was born in December 1962. If you do the math, you can figure out why they married. The photo of my parent's wedding day shows my father wearing a tie and my mother wearing a skirt and matching jacket. The photo was taken in front of the King County, Seattle, WA courthouse. Neither of my parents looks happy in that photo.

After they married, my parents bought the house next door to my maternal grandparents. I'm not entirely sure why because my mother and her mother were not close.

My parents moved into that house and lived together until they divorced in 1969. When they divorced, my mother moved out with my sister and me, leaving the house to my father.
I am unsure why that was the arrangement. At the time of my parents' divorce, my mother, at the age of 28, did not have a driver's license. She didn't work outside the home. She lived next door to her parents. So, why would she move out, taking her young girls with her, when she split from my father?

During the short number of years my parents were married, my paternal grandmother, Grandma Mary, lived with us off and on. She would often babysit my sister and me while my parents were out. My sister was Grandma Mary's clear favorite grandchild, and, my mother once told me, when asked why she clearly preferred my older sister over me, Grandma Mary answered, "I only have room in my heart for one grandchild." That favoritism came with a cost. When my parents left Grandma Mary in charge, I was typically ordered to my room. I remember peeking out of my bedroom door and seeing Grandma Mary in the living room, sharing her cigarettes with my sister. Lori was 4 years old. I don't remember any occasion when Grandma Mary was sober. Growing up in a family of alcoholics, I categorized them into one of two categories – happy drunks or mean drunks. Grandma Mary was a mean drunk. My mother was also a mean drunk. In thinking that humans recreate what they are accustomed to in childhood, I imagine my father choosing my mother was meant to be. My mother was much like her mother-in-law; her own desires always came before those of her children, she was often angry, and she was prone to violence.

I have very few memories of my childhood. I've worked with therapists over the years who suggested I revive those memories. I've not been interested in doing so. The reason? My older sister has clear memories of our childhood. She's experienced mental illness and addiction issues throughout her life, beginning in her teen years. I know the root of addiction is pain. I have no desire to remember much of the pain.

Me, on the left, and Lori, on the right, circa 1969

Growing up in the 1960s and 70s with alcoholic parents, I learned early in life that certain things must be kept secret. My mother was an alcoholic and physically abusive, and she dated and married alcoholic men who were abusive to her two young daughters. As a result, I didn't invite friends over when I was a small child until I moved out of my mother's house at 17. I didn't want any of my friends to know what my home life was like.

My parents divorced when I was 4, and my older sister Lori was 6. My paternal grandmother (Mary) died at the age of 56. I was told she'd not seen a doctor since my father was born years prior to her death. Grandma Mary was married seven times, twice to the same man. The only husband of hers I remember was my Grandpa Ray. He was the man that adopted my father and gave him the last name of Nelson. Grandpa Ray was an alcoholic. However, my memories of him are pleasant. At the end of his life, Grandpa Ray lived in a small apartment in northwest Washington State. My first husband and I would visit him often.

Grandpa Ray, Dad, and me (holding Corey), 1991

Grandpa Ray thought I was my mother on our last few visits. He would ask me about my girls (my sister Lori and me), thinking I was my mother. Grandpa Ray is one of the very few relatives I remember with fondness. I played along when he thought I was my mother during those visits. Grandpa Ray was a good man – how he got involved with my Grandma Mary is a mystery.

After my Grandma Mary divorced my Grandpa Ray, she took up with several interesting men. The only one that sticks in my memory is a man I remember as Bob LeMaux. Bob was Native American, and when he would drink (which was every day), he would chant Native American songs, complete with drumming his hands on the table. When I think back to the racist comments my father made about every ethnicity other than whites, I wonder what he thought of Bob LeMaux.

As in most families, many stories are rumored to be true. One of those stories holds that my Grandma Mary wanted a daughter, so she dressed my father as a girl when he was an infant. I've also been told that my Grandma Mary would take her infant son with her to the bar and leave him sitting behind the bar while she drank and interacted with the other patrons. In addition, Grandma Mary had bluebirds tattooed on her thighs, something very risqué for a woman in the 1940s.

My father was very close to several of his cousins from his mother's family. Dad used to go fishing and camping with his cousins, the extended family got together for a Christmas party every year, and the cousins would have contests about who could stand the strongest hot sauce.

My paternal biological grandfather was a man named Thomas Moore. As the family story goes, my Grandma Mary met Thomas Moore and soon became pregnant with my father. Thomas Moore was in the navy, and it is rumored that he wanted to marry my grandmother. I am not sure why that didn't happen, but I am sure that Thomas Moore dodged a bullet by not marrying my Grandma Mary.

Chapter 2:

Post-Divorce: Living with a Single Mom

"I ...understand how a parent might hit a child- it's because you can look into their eyes and see a reflection of yourself that you wish you hadn't."

— Jodi Picoult

Though she was 28 years old at the time of the divorce, my mother didn't have a driver's license. Having gone from living with her parents to living with my father, my mother had never lived independently and was fully unprepared for life as a single mother. Working as a cocktail waitress and exotic dancer, my mother frequently brought men home from the bar. At the tender ages of 4 and 6, my sister and I cared for ourselves – making our own meals and getting by with little, if any, parental supervision.

My mother thought it would be inappropriate for my sister and me to see a strange man in her bed each morning when we got ourselves up to make breakfast. So – mother would have the date from the night before move to the couch before her girls got up. I'm not sure why she thought that was more acceptable... but I guess it was a small thing that made her feel somewhat better about herself. What I remember most about those mornings was that my sister and I became quite good at communicating silently, using our hands and facial expressions. We didn't want to wake the strange man on the couch.

My maternal grandmother Eleanor loved my sister and me, but she held a traditional mind view of what a family should look like. To that end, she encouraged our mother to find a man to marry so that my sister and I would have a father.

During her years as a single mother, my mother frequently left my sister and me with our maternal grandmother. Though we loved Grandma Eleanor deeply, our grandfather – my mother's stepfather – was a different story. Grandma Eleanor had my mother out of wedlock in 1942. This was a big deal – she was from a strict Catholic family. Her father told his daughters there were only two ways to leave the family home. One was to be married, and the other was to join the nunnery. Grandma Eleanor bucked those rules and left her home in North Dakota as a young single woman with her sister Barbara. The two young women left the family farm and traveled to various places in the United States. There are stories of them living in Nevada and California, with my grandmother working as a waitress and my great-aunt working as a baker.

At some point in 1942, my grandmother became pregnant with my mother. This was a big taboo, and, in my years of research and the available DNA websites in recent years, I've found that my maternal biological grandfather was a married man.

Grandma Eleanor married her husband, Pete, when my mother was 5. For her first 5 years, my mother lived with her aunt Barbara, my grandmother's sister. My aunt Barbara was married, and she and her husband found themselves unable to have children. Having my mother live with them created a happy family.

Grandpa Pete was a Merchant Marine. He spent months away from home, and I remember the times he was away as being the happiest at my grandparent's home. My grandmother had two more children with her husband. My uncle was born when my mother was 5, and my aunt was born when my mother was in high school. My grandmother worked as a waitress these years, and my mother looked after her younger siblings.

When he was home, Grandpa Pete was to be avoided. "Come sit on my lap, doll!" he would yell when he saw my sister or me. Sitting on Grandpa Pete's lap was unpleasant, and I remember avoiding him as much as possible growing up. Some years later, when I had my own children, I made sure they knew that being close to Grandpa Pete was to be avoided and to speak up when he would attempt to gather them into his lap. My grandparent's home had a tall, skinny closet in the hallway. I loved to hide in that closet, especially when Grandpa Pete was home.

My grandmother Eleanor was German. She wasn't very affectionate though I know she loved my sister and me. My grandmother taught me to bake. One of her well-known recipes was for red velvet cake. My memories of that cake are that it was the best-tasting thing in this world. When I was a young adult, I asked my grandmother for the recipe. She refused and said, "Maybe when you're older." Unfortunately, I never got that recipe.

After retiring from the Merchant Marines, Grandpa Pete worked as a maintenance person at a local Catholic church and school where he and my grandmother were members. After multiple complaints from parents asserting improper touching of their children, Grandpa Pete was let go from his position. After that, he retired. My grandparents were placed in assisted living facilities toward the end of their lives. They were in different facilities, though I'm not sure why that was the case. Grandpa Pete was in a facility with both men and women residents. One day, the family of one of the female residents reported they could not locate their mother. The woman had severe dementia, and the facility worried she'd wandered off. It turns out my grandfather had the woman in his room the entire time she was missing and claimed she wanted to be there. The woman's family threatened to sue the facility, and my Grandpa Pete was moved to a men-only care home.

My mother and my sister were far closer than I ever was with my mother. As I write that, I wonder whether they were closer or my sister simply wished they were. My mother shared details about her adult life with my sister that she didn't share with me. Honestly, I'm happy my mother didn't share those details. There are things I think are inappropriate to share with one's children. Though my Grandpa Pete was not my mother's biological father, my mother wasn't told that until her 18th birthday. On that day, her parents shared with my mother that Grandpa Pete was not her biological father. Still, my grandmother would not tell my mother the identity of her biological father. At the end of my mother's 18th birthday day, Grandpa Pete entered her bedroom and told her he was there to help her become a woman. My mother described the event as "making love," a term I've always hated. Given our mother's inability to show love and affection to her children, my sister was easy prey for our grandfather. Many years later, as an adult, my sister spoke up about the sexual abuse she endured. Like many families where abuse occurs, everyone was shocked and outraged at the accusation, and my sister spent some years shunned for bringing up the truth. Like many families where sexual abuse occurs, I am certain both my mother and grandmother were aware of what was happening to Lori all those years.

Chapter 3:
New Stepdad

"Most children would rather preserve the fantasy of a loving connection with their fathers and mothers, at all costs, even if it costs them their self-esteem. When you're three or seven years old, it's less frightening to think of yourself as an unlovable, disappointing screwup than to recognize the fact that you're living with a monster."

-Keith Ablow

My mother met her second husband in the bar where she worked as a bartender and exotic dancer. Though I was very young, I remember her costumes with skimpy bottoms and simple stickers over her nipples. After a few years of bringing home random men most nights, my mother met Gary. He was a car wash attendant and frequent patron of the bar where my mother worked and danced. Like all the men my mother ever spent time with, he was an alcoholic. My mother told me once that she married her second husband because her mother told her she should get a father for my sister and me. Once she married Gary, we moved into a series of crappy rental homes. We rarely stayed one entire year in a residence before moving. As a result, I was a freshman in high school before I finished the school year at the same school.

My mother was an angry woman. When I think back on her life, I wonder if she was that way because she found she had to put the needs of others ahead of her own at times. This is especially so when it came to her children. She was a selfish woman who should not have had children. I think she would have been happier without children, and I think her children would have been better off with another mother.

My mother's anger could often be triggered by fights with my stepdad. There were many occasions when the two of them would be very drunk and start fighting. My mother was proud of a painting hanging over the fireplace in one of our rental homes. The painting was of my mother, done in chalky pastels. She had a flip-up hairstyle, and I imagine it was painted in the late 60s or early 70s. During one of their intense fights, my stepdad grabbed the painting from above the fireplace and threw it into the fireplace. As it went up in flames, my mother attacked him. After that, physical fighting was common between the two of them. My mother would have mascara streaming down her face, and her husband would call her "Queenie." I don't know where that name came from, but wow, did it fire up my mother.

During the first years of her second marriage, my mother ran an in-home daycare. I look back on this with a twisted sense of amusement and wonder. My mother was quick to use her hands, or any nearby object, to hit one of her daughters – how she became licensed as a daycare provider escapes me.

My mother and her husband believed in corporal punishment. To that end, they had a leather belt they'd folded in half, then duct-taped together. This was their spanking tool, and my sister and I were often recipients. I cannot honestly remember what event would take place for one of us to earn that belt. As a parent myself, I've often said – if the memory of the punishment outweighs the memory of the infraction, the punishment was far too severe.

We were living in a rental house in Seattle when I threw that belt behind the hot water heater. My mother and her husband searched for days. My sister and I were both punished because they knew one of us would break and tell them where the belt was. My sister didn't know.

She would have broken down and given up the location if she had. Lori was always quick to cry and cower, which satisfied our mother. My power resided in my ability to NOT tell where the belt was. I took the punishment and refused to talk. That was my way with my mother. My only power was my ability not to give in. To not show emotion. To not cry. Of course, that infuriated my mother and typically resulted in even harsher punishments for me.

I've often wondered what the reaction was when some future owner replaced that hot water tank and found that duct tape-wrapped belt.

We lived in a tiny apartment at one point after my mother married her second husband. My sister and I shared a small room and slept in the same bed. In a drunken rage, my mother broke a dinner plate over my head one night. She also used a fly swatter to hit my sister and me. I once got that fly swatter so hard across my face that it left a red mark for days.

I don't remember anyone asking me about that at school, but that was a different time from today – teachers weren't required to report abuse, and I imagine many of them didn't want to become involved.

My mother's ability to appear so calm and collected when we were out in public was interesting. My sister and I were warned about proper behavior whenever we went out. For example, my sister and I could not accept a snack or treat from anyone unless our mother said it was okay. Lori and I would sit quietly when we visited others, and if either of us did something that was not allowed, our mother would give us "the look."

I was 8, and my sister was 10 years old when our little brother was born. From his first days home from the hospital, our brother was my sister's and my sole responsibility. We lived about a mile away from the nearest laundromat. So, after several glasses of wine, my mother would nap, and my sister and I would place our infant brother and a basket of dirty laundry in a wagon and walk to the laundromat to do the laundry. A package of Doritos was 25 cents back then. My sister and I would share the chips and watch our brother until the laundry was done. When my mother was out of cigarettes, she would give Lori or me the money to get her a pack from the vending machine at the laundromat.

A friend used the term "free-range parenting" in passing just a couple of years ago. As I pondered the term, I realized it was a good descriptor of my mother's parenting style. "Seen, but not heard" was her mantra regarding children. Her alcoholic bouts of rage knew no bounds, and my sister and I both bear physical scars.

During one heated moment of anger, my mother told me that if abortion had been legal the year I was born, I wouldn't be here.

My mother's second husband had trouble keeping a job. Shortly after he married my mother, my stepdad took a job as a maintenance person at the apartment complex his parents managed. My mother used to scream at him about his inability to provide an income for the family. She eventually took a job as a telephone operator with the local telephone company. Memories of the operator job always make me laugh, for my mother's telephone voice was vastly different from the one she used at home. I remember several times when my mother would scream at my sister or me, then the telephone would ring. Then, my mother would transform from a screaming banshee to a calm woman as she picked up the phone and used her most pleasant voice, "Hello?"

Christmases were not fun holidays in my home. We had a tradition when it came to decorating the tree. My mother would string the lights, and my sister and I would hang the ornaments. Then, my stepdad would start with the tinsel. He placed one strand at a time. It was always Elvis Presley's music playing at a very loud volume. In the earlier years, Lori and I were made to hang tinsel on the tree. Neither of us had the patience to hang one string at a time, so we would go behind the tree and throw our handfuls onto the tree. When caught, our stepdad was not happy. After swatting both of us, he sent my sister and me to our room. What he didn't seem to realize was that was where we wanted to be, away from the chaos of drunken parents fighting with one another. I've never been a fan of Elvis Presley's music and never placed tinsel on my tree as an adult.

In true form, my mother soon looked to find herself in another man. She had several affairs, mainly with men she worked with, while married to her second husband. I remember she would go on work trips out of town, and when her husband mentioned that my mother didn't answer the phone in her hotel room when he called, my mother would tell him,

"I must not have heard the ring because the television was too loud." I highly doubt her husband believed that excuse.

My father offered to pay for a trip to Hawaii when I graduated from high school. The catch was that I had to have a friend come along, and the friend had to pay their own way. Unfortunately, my best friend could not come up with the funds, so my mother stepped in and joined me on that trip.

On our first night on the island, my mother and I went to the hotel bar. The drinking age in Hawaii was 18 at the time, so I could sit in the bar and enjoy a glass of wine. The piano player was the typical lounge player; he had a slick appearance playing to the drunken tourist crowd. On a break, the piano player approached the table where my mother and I were seated. "You two must be sisters?" he asked. Seriously? My mother slurred, "Oh no! This is my daughter!" The piano player said something about how she looked so young and beautiful. I left shortly after that and went to our hotel room. My mother returned around 8 am, disheveled and hung over. She spent most of that week in the hotel bar and didn't return to our room any of the nights we were there.

Chapter 4:
Next Stepdad

My sister was a rebel. She and her friends drank alcohol and experimented with drugs. My sister was thrown out of the house after an unpleasant fight where my mother slapped my sister's bare thigh with a hot, greasy spatula. She has a burn scar that resembles a waffle on her thigh to this day.

I remember the fear I felt, knowing I would be the only target of attention once my sister was gone. Being invisible was my highest skill up to that point in my life, and it is hard to be invisible when you have no sister to hide behind. My stepdad understood my predicament. I remember him saying, "You are in the spotlight now." My sister was 15 years old when she was thrown out and she dropped out of high school. She was just at the beginning of her freshman year and never returned to school.

Once my sister was gone, my mother and her second husband soon parted ways. It turns out my mother was having an affair with a married co-worker. The co-worker's wife contacted my stepdad to inform him of the affair. They split up soon after that, and my stepdad moved across the state to be closer to his parents. After my sister was gone, the care of my younger brother was left to me. If I wanted to make plans, I was responsible for arranging and paying for a babysitter or bringing my brother along. My mother soon married her third husband and the two of them liked to drink in the bars rather than at home, as had been the habit she had with her second husband. This meant they would be gone from early morning until the wee hours, only to sleep for a few hours and perform the same routine.

I moved out of my mother's home when I was 17. Truth be told, I would have gone sooner, but I couldn't leave my little brother behind. The summer I moved out, my brother went to spend time with his dad. Not surprisingly, when it came time for my brother to return to my mother's house, he did not want to go. My sister and I picked our brother up at his father's house, and he cried all the way home. This was a 6-hour drive. Once we got home, my mother called her ex-husband, and both agreed my brother should go live with his dad. That was probably the best parenting move my mother ever made, for it allowed my brother to grow up away from our mother, without the experience of her physical abuse. She didn't make this decision based on what was best for my brother; she knew she would no longer have to deal with having children at home, and my brother's father agreed she would not have to pay child support.

Several years after being out of my mother's home, I asked her why she'd exposed her daughters to such abuse as we grew up. Her second husband constantly told my sister she was stupid and would never amount to anything. He told me I was ugly and should focus on my intelligence because my looks would get me nowhere. I brought up the constant stream of strange men and our grandfather's sexual abuse. I wasn't looking for an apology; I just wanted to know why any mother would subject her children to these events.

My mother's answer was, "I did the best with what I had to work with at the time." I've often said that my parenting skills have included thinking about what my mother would do... then doing the exact opposite. There have been many times as a parent that I've struggled with knowing what I should do. Unfortunately, my role model was not a reliable source for answers. As a result, I've had to turn to some close friends for advice over the years.

After moving out of my mother's home, I lived independently for a year. Then I met Vince. He was older than me. My relationship with Vince was tumultuous at times, and being so young, my heart was broken easily.

Chapter 5:

The Adult Daughter

"When you grieve toxic, abusive parents, you don't just grieve the abuse, you grieve everything you didn't have."

— *Lily Hope Lucario*

Once I'd moved out of my mother's home, I realized I still had no freedom from her. She was a pro at manipulation and had a knack for saying incredibly cruel things. I didn't spend much time with her, and she eventually moved out of Washington State. Before she moved, my mother invited me to her home to give me some items she did not want to take with her. She opened a cedar trunk and pulled out a few family photos. I took those. Then, she pulled out a handful of homemade items my siblings and I had given her over the years. The funky Christmas ornaments, clay ashtrays, that sort of thing. At that time in my life, I had only my first child. When he was three months old, his daycare provider gave me a potholder for Mother's Day with my son's handprint and footprint on it. Though my oldest son is now in his 30s, I cherished that gift then and still have it today. At first, I looked at those childhood creations and had a spark that maybe my mother wasn't so awful if she'd kept these things for so many years. When I asked her if she wanted to keep any of them for herself, she said, "I didn't want any of them in the first place and completely forgot they were in here until I began packing." Quick snap back to reality for me and that spark was out. I didn't take any of the items. Each of them held a memory of the child who created it, handing it to their mother with pride and joy, so wanting their mother to love them. None of those memories were for me.

My mother moved to Texas in 1991. After that, she moved to Missouri, then she moved to Florida in 1998. I didn't visit her in any of those places. However, my mother would periodically fly back to Washington State to visit her parents. Her last trip to visit her parents was in September 2001. She came to town to help pack up her parent's items as my grandparents were being moved to an assisted living facility. My mother wasn't the type of daughter who took great care of her parents. In fact, I remember my mother regretted making the trip at all because she was delayed in flying home to Florida due to the 9/11 terrorist attacks closing all airports for a few days.

Though I visited Florida a few times to take my kids to Disneyworld during the years my mother lived in that state, I took great care to be sure my mother didn't know I was in town because I had no interest in visiting with her.

For some reason, I felt compelled to call my mother on her birthday and Mother's Day as a young adult. I remember when the internet first became a thing, and everyone had an America Online (AOL) account. When it came time for one of those obligatory calls to my mother, I would log into AOL and, if I saw my mother was also online, I would take that opportunity to call her. Her phone calls would go to her answering machine when she was online. This trick allowed me to leave a message without talking to my mother.

I would purchase Mother's Day cards for my mother. It was always a challenge to find cards that weren't sappy, "You're the best mom ever!" It seems that cards for mothers lean toward the assumption that the child loves their parent and appreciates the parenting they've been given. I would often buy a blank card, write "Happy Mother's Day" inside, and sign my name. There. The obligation was done but I didn't have to be fake about it. As I got older, I stopped with the cards. It felt like a charade and, once I had my own children, I had no time for that.

One summer my sister reached out to our mother to ask if my niece could spend a month in Florida with my mother. My mother wrote back to say she would agree, but only if my oldest daughter would come along as well. My mother wanted the two girls to entertain themselves for the month so there wouldn't be much for my mother to do. My niece was 9 and my daughter was 8. As soon as I got the request, I knew there was no way on God's green earth that my daughter would spend a month with my mother. I tried a few lame excuses... can't afford the plane ticket, my daughter won't be able to spend a month away from me, etc. My mother saw through those excuses and called me out – "Why won't you send Mallory to Florida for a month?" OK, truth time. "My daughter has no idea what it is like to have an adult intoxicated 24 hours a day, 7 days a week. She has never seen an adult physically fight with another adult. She's never experienced police responding to a domestic violence call. My daughter has never been fearful to be in her own home. She has never needed to find a safe place to hide. I will not allow that to change."

My mother responded by telling me that she believed I thought I was better than her. I answered before I thought it through. I should have ignored her comment. Instead, I said, "Yes, I am better than you." After that, we didn't communicate with one another for several years.

Many years later, my mother asked to have her three children with her for Easter. Mother was living in Florida. My brother and his wife were living in Boston, and my sister was living with my mother, providing in-home care for my great-aunt. I bought airline tickets. I dreaded going. The day we were to fly to Florida came, I told my husband, "I just can't do this. I have no desire to see her. She will be drunk; everyone will be stressed." My husband said, "Then, let's not go." So, my brother, his wife, and their young son went. I did not. I sent my mother a message that I'd thrown my back out and couldn't sit on the plane that long. That was not true. Wow... was she angry. I received several messages about how inconsiderate I was, how I didn't appreciate all she'd done for me, how my siblings were much better children than I was. I didn't answer any of those messages.

My brother and his wife were married in 2008. I'd planned to go to the wedding; I booked a hotel room and arranged for time off from work. My mother was going to fly in from where she lived in Florida to Oregon, where the wedding was held. The night she was to leave, she arrived at the airport in Florida very drunk. The flight staff refused to allow her to board, due to her intoxication. She was forced to go home and fly out the next day. When I heard that, I had a burst of anxiety. The thought of spending time with my mother, especially when she is so drunk and denied boarding a plane, made me feel physically ill. I cancelled my hotel reservations. I didn't attend my brother's wedding. My sister was there and shared a photo taken of my mother. My mother's eyes were mostly closed and the lopsided smile on her face gave it away – my mother was bombed in that photo.

My mother, at my brother's wedding, 2008

My mother was diagnosed with bladder cancer in 2011. Shortly after, she married her fourth husband, a man I had never met. She said she married him so she would have someone close by to make healthcare decisions for her if she couldn't make them herself. My mother chose to undergo chemotherapy and radiation but wouldn't have surgery. She worried that the possibility of an external bladder would make her unattractive. As my mother's condition worsened, she contacted me on the phone. The caller ID identified her, so I let the call go to voicemail. She told me she would like to talk to me because she felt her end was near. I did not return the phone call.

A few months later, it was a Saturday night in December 2012. I was attending a Christmas work party with a group of colleagues when my cell phone rang. I didn't recognize the number, but I answered the call anyway. It was my mother's husband, Frank. He said, "You should call your mother; I didn't think she will live much longer." I thanked him for the call and returned to the Christmas party, where I sang karaoke. The next morning, Frank called to let me know my mother had died. I said, "I'm sorry for your loss."

The next day was Monday, a workday. In a meeting with my boss, she asked about my weekend. I don't know why I said it, but I told her, "My mother died this weekend." The look on my boss' face was one of horror- "Why are you working today when your mother just died?" she asked me. I was flustered and embarrassed. How does one admit they have fewer feelings for their mother than for the local grocery clerk? I told my boss, "My mother and I were not close. Please don't mention this to my colleagues, as I don't want to have to explain my lack of grieving to anyone." My boss had a large bouquet of flowers delivered to my home and a sympathy card. I took the flowers to a nearby retirement home and gave them to the front desk as a Christmas gift from me for their residents. It felt wrong to keep this beautiful bouquet of flowers sent to me as a gesture of condolence for a person I would not miss.

I have been accused of punishing my mother by not reaching out to her in her final days. I don't see it that way at all. I am guessing she wanted absolution. She was raised Catholic, after all. I am guessing she wanted to apologize for her "mothering" to ask me to excuse/forgive her behavior. Maybe I'm wrong. At the time of this writing, it has been 10 years since my mother died. In all that time, I cannot imagine anything she could have said to me that would make a difference in my life. I didn't need any apologies, and I think if she hadn't offered one, I would have been angry. I didn't need any explanations; if she had tried to defend her actions, I would have been angry. I cannot think of a scenario where I would have come away from a conversation with my mother feeling peace or comfort. It was not my responsibility to provide her with absolution. Maybe she just wanted to say goodbye. I'd found my peace with my mother years earlier, and that did not include me talking with her in her last days.

In the weeks after my mother died, her husband reached out to ask me if there was anything of my mother's that I would like. I told him no. He had her cremated and wanted to know if I wanted any of her ashes. In my head, I was thinking, "Dear God, NO." I said, "No, thank you for the offer, but I don't want them." I then began receiving boxes from my mother's husband. These boxes contained photo albums from her work parties with people I'd never met. Some knickknacks that meant absolutely nothing to me.

Upon receipt of a third box of things from Frank, I called him and asked him to stop. I told him to save the money on shipping and donate any items he did not want to a local thrift store. I never heard from Frank again. As I write this, it occurs to me that I don't know what Frank's last name was.

Chapter 6:

In A New York Minute

"Your new life is going to cost you your old one. It's going to cost you your comfort zone and your sense of direction. It's going to cost you relationships and friends. It's going to cost you being liked and understood."

- Brianna Wiest

Vince was eight years older than me. He was Italian, and his family was "connected." As in... to the mafia. I was 19 years old. Vince was an amateur weightlifter, and part of his routine was to use steroids. Vince's family lived in New York, and Vince decided he would move home to be closer to his family. This was in the mid-1980s, and I did what many teenage girls did then – I made Vince a mix tape of songs about broken hearts. Tina Turner's *You Better Be Good to Me,* Stevie Nicks and Tom Petty's *Stop Draggin' My Heart Around.* This was the first time Vince broke my heart. After a few days, he asked me if I would like to move with him to New York. I thought he was the love of my life, so I packed my stuff and my dog, and we drove across the country.

Vince and me, Circa 1984

Vince's family was not excited about him bringing home an Irish Catholic girl. I didn't know the rules of proper "respect," and the family rejected me. So, I got a job right away and learned how to drive in New York – let's just say it is an aggressive way of driving.

Vince and I got engaged; he bought me a lovely diamond ring. We never made plans for a wedding, and after two years of living with him in New York, I was considering leaving and returning home to Seattle. I wasn't happy and felt very uncomfortable with Vince's family. Vince was a bit paranoid about the government and the possibility that we would need to go "underground" to protect ourselves. To that end, he stockpiled guns. He got both of us fake passports in case we needed to make a disappearance. On my fake passport, I was Lisa Peterson.

When we moved to New York, Vince and I drove my Jeep. I loved that car and have fond memories of taking the top off the Jeep and the off-road adventures in the mountains of Washington State with my dog in the passenger seat. My personalized license plate for the Jeep was "Chrissy." Because I took the Jeep off-road often, I had a roll cage installed so that, in the event the Jeep rolled, the occupants would be better protected.

Once we got to New York, the Jeep was not practical. With its soft top, the Jeep doors could not be locked, so it was a constant fear that it would be stolen. Vince sold the Jeep to a high school friend shortly after we moved. About a year later, he bought it back from his friend. He knew I missed it, so he gave me the keys for my birthday. As part of my birthday gift, Vince added rabbit skin seat covers when he bought the Jeep back for me.

Vince worked about 20 miles from our apartment, and one day, he didn't come home from work at his regular time. I opened a bottle of wine and had a glass, knowing his tardiness was uncommon. It was around 9 pm that I received a telephone call from Vince's dad – Vince had been involved in a car accident and was in the hospital.

Vince was driving my Jeep that night as he left work. The police report stated that another car started to merge into his lane, and Vince overcompensated. This caused the Jeep to roll several times before coming to rest on the side of the highway. Though the Jeep was equipped with lap seat belts, Vince wasn't wearing his. When the police and paramedics arrived, they found Vince with his head smashed against the roll bar.

Vince's family picked me up and drove me to the hospital, where we found Vince in the intensive care unit. His left arm was in a soft cast – we were told the arm was shattered in the accident. His head was wrapped in bandages and he was hooked up to several machines. We were told he'd sustained an injury to his head and that brain tissue was exposed at the site of the injury. The date was January 22, 1987. It was cold and snowing outside.

Over the next five days, Vince's condition held stable. He didn't wake. His large family came to visit him, and I was reminded of a conversation Vince and I had several months prior when one of his family members was terminally ill and on life support. Vince and I agreed that neither of us would want to be kept alive via machines should we be in the same condition. I approached Vince's father and shared that conversation with him. Vince's dad was a strong man, an unemotional man. He was the father of five children and the boss of a number of operations in the Bronx. He tried to hold back the tears as he heard me out. Then he went to the doctors in the ICU and told them he did not want his son kept alive on machines.

Vince's family arranged to pick up the damaged Jeep. I remember it being towed into their driveway and looking inside. The rabbit skin seat cover on the driver's side was soaked in blood.

Five days. Vince lived five days in the ICU of that hospital in the Bronx. On day five, I was at his bedside when he flexed his bicep on his left arm. The broken arm. He flexed that bicep numerous times, and I cried, thinking the message was that I should be strong because he would pull through. Vince died just a few minutes after the last flex of his bicep. His message was not for me to be strong because he would pull through. It was for me to be strong because he would not.

That was the last time he broke my heart. I was 22 years old.

The weeks following Vince's death were fast-paced. Family from all over the world flew to New York for what I was to learn was a wake. For an entire week, Vince's remains were viewable in an open casket in the funeral home while the immediate family sat nearby and visitors paid their respects. The funeral home placed a wig on Vince's head due to the damage he sustained in the accident. I remember thinking he would hate the hairstyle. The smell of flowers was overwhelming. It was several years before the smell of flowers was something I could enjoy. I remember smiling, hugging, shaking hands... and telling people I was all right. The most memorable visit was from a woman who said, "It's a good thing you are so young. You will be able to find another partner." That, by the way, was nowhere near comforting.

I took one of the flowers from Vince's casket. It was a white chrysanthemum. I flattened and dried that flower and placed it in a shadow box. I added a photo of the two of us and other items that reminded me of Vince.

I needed to dispose of Vince's arsenal of guns. They were owned legally, but I could not sell them. One of Vince's friends was a corrections officer. He came over, took possession of the guns, and gave me the money he felt they were worth. I kept mine and Vince's fake passports for several moves though I lost them and that shadow box in one of my many moves over the next few years.

After Vince died, I moved back to the Pacific Northwest, where my family was and where I felt most at home.

Chapter 7:

John

"At any given moment, you have the power to say: this is not how the story is going to end."

- Christine Mason Miller

Once I moved back to Seattle, I started working in a medical office. I didn't sleep much, and I drank a lot of alcohol. As a result, I lost a lot of weight, and my hair began to fall out. Upon the recommendation of a co-worker, I started counseling at a local community center. My counselor was a young man who had no experience with grief counseling.

His biggest contribution to my therapy was to suggest that I carry a large rock in a backpack and go hiking. The idea was that I would think of the rock as a burden and, one day, I would be able to leave the rock behind, symbolizing my ability to let the grief go.

My short-term memory was gone, which was incredibly frustrating for someone like me. I remember driving to the local mall to go shopping. When I came out of the mall, I could not remember where I parked my car. I sat down on the steps of the store and cried. A security person walked up and asked how he could help. "I can't find my car," I answered. He asked me, "What kind of car do you drive?" My answer was, "I don't remember."

A few months after moving back to the Pacific Northwest, a high school friend of mine introduced me to her cousin. John was the same age as me, he was a high school dropout, and had a fondness for cocaine. When I met John, he was living in his car. I saw him as someone I could save, and I think he saw me as someone who could save him, so we began dating. It was 1987. I was not sleeping. I was at an unhealthy low weight. I needed a distraction.

Within a few months of dating, John and I decided to move in together. We rented a small apartment. I worked in Seattle as a medical assistant, and he worked for his father's roofing company. Eventually, John began working for himself, and I helped him form his own company building custom construction homes.

One night, John asked me what I thought I would be doing in five years. I said, "Well, I will be married to you..." I'm not entirely sure why I said that, but it became our engagement. We planned our wedding to take place on July 16, 1988.

John was not Catholic, but many of my family members were. John and I met with the priest of my grandmother's church. It became clear that John's conversion to Catholicism would be lengthy and that John wasn't very interested... so we chose a local non-denominational church for our wedding. My wedding was designed to be perfect — amazing dress, fantastic decorations. We hired a band and had a swan ice sculpture on the table at the reception. I still couldn't stand the smell of fresh flowers; they reminded me of pain and grief. So, I made all the bouquets out of silk flowers. The day and evening were amazing.

My father bought us a trip to Hawaii as a wedding gift. Ironically, it was in the same hotel where my mother and I had our room when I graduated from high school.

Shortly after John and I married, we rented a house from my mother and her third husband. The plan was for John and me to purchase the house once we had enough money for the down payment. That day came, and we moved forward with purchasing the house.

Not long after purchasing the house, I wanted to add a baby to our family. John was in agreement, so we started trying to become pregnant. Things weren't working out as we had hoped, and I found myself more and more depressed with each month that would go by without me becoming pregnant. John and I visited a fertility specialist. That doctor put me on a medication that would increase our odds of becoming parents. John was a twin, and twins ran in his family. I remember fearing the possibility of a multiple birth, once on fertility medications.

John and me, Hawaiian honeymoon, July 1988

I found myself pregnant in the fall of 1990. I was thrilled. Buying maternity clothes was fun, even though the clothes were so "cute" in those days. Though I was never close to my mother, I remember excitedly telling her I was pregnant. Her response was, "I didn't want any of my own children, so don't expect me to take care of yours!"

I worked until the day I went into labor with my oldest son. John and I spent 24 hours at the hospital before our firstborn appeared. I've never felt love like what I felt when I looked upon Corey's face. My grandmother brought fresh flowers to the hospital. It was the first time since before Vince's death that the smell of flowers made me smile. The flowers were hyacinths, and the strong smell was almost overwhelming in that small hospital room.

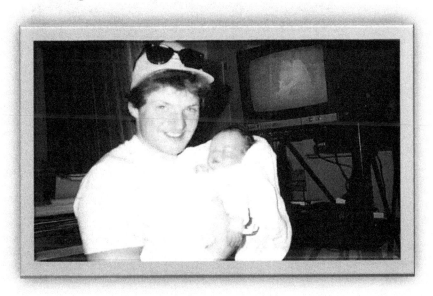

John, with newborn Corey, March 1991

After our son was born, John and I decided to move to a larger house. John was a licensed general contractor by then and planned to build our new home. John would take our son with him to the worksite and let him "help" build the house.

My second child was due in August 1993. After the long labor with my first child, I chose to have an all-natural birth the second time. I hired a labor coach and sought care with my primary care physician. Back in those days, primary care docs still delivered babies. My labor with my second child was vastly different from that of my first. I felt in control; I felt empowered. I refer to that birth as the best of all my five children.

John and Corey working on our new house, 1993

I wanted to name my daughter "Riley," but John wasn't a fan of the name. So, we settled on "Mallory" for our daughter.

Our house construction was completed just after our daughter was born in August 1993. It was a very nice home, with three bedrooms plus an office. Ours was a perfect life. Once my oldest daughter arrived, my family was complete.

Ours was one of the first houses built in the new neighborhood, so the first couple of years there were incredibly quiet. As more houses were built, the neighborhood became busier. John and I became friends with neighbors, and we would have block parties for the 4th of July, and Christmas time tree-trimming parties at our home. Because our living room had a 20' vaulted ceiling, our Christmas tree was always. very tall.

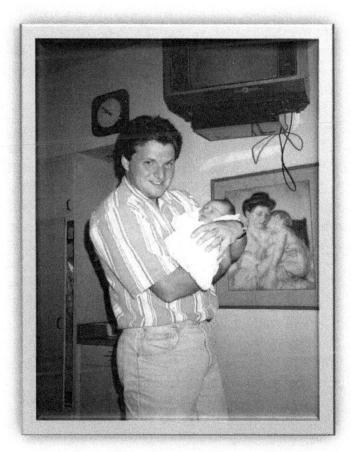

John holding Mallory, August 1993

John loved Halloween; I think it was his favorite holiday. We would buy 20-25 pumpkins, and John would intricately carve each one. He would make a scarecrow for the front lawn and cover the trees and porch in "spiderwebs." I made homemade costumes for the kids. One year, Corey was Robin Hood, and Mallory was a princess. Thanksgiving has always been my favorite holiday, and I invited family and friends over to enjoy a feast each year.

Our family tradition was to spend Christmas Eve with my dad and my stepmother. John and I would get the kids dressed up, and we would head to Seattle for dinner and fun with my father and family. Neither my father nor my stepmother were cooks, so Christmas Eve dinner was always something pretty simple. My favorite was my dad's red clam chowder. Though it is a very simple recipe, I am glad my dad shared it with me before he died.

The first five years after marrying John hold many happy memories. Backyard bar-b-ques with family and friends. I painted stenciled flowers on the bathroom walls. John built a backyard play climber for the kids. Because John built the house himself, he was able to incorporate some fun things that we would not likely have been able to afford otherwise. We had a walk-in closet in the master bathroom and a large jetted soaking tub. John installed a large hot tub in the backyard, complete with a gazebo for cover and a built-in stereo system.

Our neighborhood was adjacent to a golf course, and John volunteered to be a golf marshal. He would take our son with him on a golf cart, collecting stray golf balls. I'm not sure who enjoyed those events more – the grown man or the young child.

Chapter 8:

John's Depression

"That's the thing about depression: A human being can survive almost anything if she sees the end in sight. But depression is so insidious, and it compounds daily, that it's impossible to ever see the end. The fog is like a cage without a key."

-Elizabeth Wurtzel

Shortly after moving to our new house, John began exhibiting symptoms of depression. In hindsight, these symptoms were obvious, but at the moment, such symptoms are not seen so clearly. John was erratic. He was often delusional, accusing me of any of a number of things. After two years of this behavior, I decided I needed to move into my own space with my young children, hoping that John would stabilize. John and I began to see a couple's therapist. That therapist recommended that John work with his own therapist and stay in couple's counseling.

I moved to an apartment close to my work, and John continued to have frequent contact with me and our children. It seemed that things would work out, and we would become a family again. Unfortunately, that all changed one night. On the night in question, I'd gone out with friends. It was a Tuesday, and we wanted to watch country line dancing at a local venue. I remember looking from the dance floor toward our table and seeing John standing there – watching my group as we danced.

After that night, John's behavior became more erratic. He continued to see and spend time with our children, but, in hindsight, that may have been a mistake. My son, then four years old, relayed to me that he, his father, and his two-year-old sister spent hours driving through town, looking for my car when they spent time with their dad. It became obvious that John was getting worse.

On August 21, 1995, I was in my apartment with my two young children. I received a call from John. He was upset. He said he was suicidal, and he hung up on me. John was living with his twin sister, and I called her repeatedly... wanting her to check on her brother. John's sister hung up on me a few times and eventually stopped answering the phone.

At 2 am, I placed my two young children in my car and drove to John's sister's house. I left a note in John's car. My note told him I loved him and wanted to make things right between us. I drove back to my apartment with my sleeping children. The next morning, I received a call from the county coroner's office. They'd responded to a call that John had committed suicide by hanging himself from his sister's backyard play set the night before.

I called my father and asked him to help me. He drove me to the coroner's office so I could complete the paperwork. I was given John's wedding ring and the watch he was wearing. The watch was a gift to him from me when we got married. My father contacted a funeral home and helped me arrange John's funeral and burial. My father was never an emotional man, but I felt supported and protected.

In the days following John's death, things were a blur. When I called John's sister, her husband answered the phone and told me, "You're not welcome here." John's family blamed me for his death, and their answer was to steal from my children and me. John's sister asked to join me for lunch to discuss John's service. I welcomed her input and thought it was a gesture that they weren't going to shun me. We met at a local Pizza Hut for lunch. As we left the restaurant, my son ran for the street. I grabbed him and asked, "What are you thinking?" He said,

"I want to die, so I can go to heaven and bring my dad back." I got my son into counseling the following week.

I found out later that John's sister was there to ensure I was preoccupied while John's family drove to the storage locker where John and I had stored many of our items. They stole photos, John's camera equipment, John's golf clubs, and John's tools. In addition, the family took our refrigerator... reminiscent of the Grinch Who Stole Christmas.

John's brother arranged to go to the job site of the house John was building at the time of his death. The brother got into the job site trailer and took John's tools. One of those tools was a nail gun John had purchased on credit just a week prior. A few days later, I received a call from my insurance company letting me know the company where John bought that nail gun had filed a lien against John's bond for the cost of the tool. I contacted John's brother and asked if he would return that tool. He agreed, but he said he didn't want to see me. He put the nail gun into his camper, parked on his property. The brother told me I could come to get the nail gun, but only during a specific time period. I worried that it was a setup, that maybe the brother would call the police to say I was stealing the tool. I didn't want my kids to witness their mother being arrested if the plan was a setup, so I arranged for a babysitter. I drove to John's brother's house and walked up to the camper. I opened the back door and found the nail gun inside. I took the item to my car, fearing a cop would pop up at any moment. No police appeared.

The next week, I packed my young children into the car and drove to the tool store. As I identified myself, the bookkeeper approached me. "Oh my, I didn't realize you and John had such young children," I asked the bookkeeper why she didn't simply contact me rather than file the lien against John's bond. She wouldn't make eye contact with me and mumbled some sort of answer. I was given a receipt for the nail gun; there was a 10% deduction off the full price for a re-stocking fee. I contacted the Better Business Bureau to file a complaint. Shortly after, I received a call from the tool company's owner. He asked for my address to refund the remaining money and told me he'd fired the bookkeeper.

The worst thing John's family stole? The video games John played with our son. One game, in particular, was Batman. John and our son played that Batman game on the Nintendo system for hours... it was father-son bonding time. When I realized John's family stole the Nintendo system and the Batman game... I was incensed. My son was devastated that his father was gone, and there was little left to remind him of his father. I remember being surprised that people could be so horrible when someone dies.

I spent a good number of days looking for that Batman game. This was before the internet and eBay. Back then, it wasn't easy to find an old game. I called pawn shops around the state of Washington, looking for that game. Eventually, I found the game in a pawn shop about six hours from where we lived. I drove to that pawn shop and sobbed as I purchased that Batman game. I'm sure the shop owner wondered what was wrong with me. But all I could think of was that I'd found the game my son needed.

Chapter 9:

New Beginnings

"We are products of our past, but we don't have to be prisoners of it."

— *Rick Warren*

After John died, I moved into a 100-year-old home with my two young children. I remember thinking that John would not want to live there – he built beautiful new homes, and the old home needed a lot of upkeep. The house was huge, and, in those early days, I left many of the rooms unfurnished. The main floor of the house had hardwood flooring, and I would sometimes roller skate in those empty rooms after my children were in bed.

Over the first few years living in that house, I would go to work all day, bring the kids home, and once they were fed and in bed, I would spend hours working in the house. This entailed removing old wallpaper, removing window coverings, and replacing light fixtures. I found a tremendous sense of healing in my work in that house. Most evenings, I would be up until 3 am painting, sanding, scraping... only to sleep a couple of hours, get the kids up and ready for the day, and start the same routine again.

During all those late nights of working, there were times when my shoulders would become so fatigued that I could no longer lift my arms. Several years later, I saw an orthopedic surgeon who asked me what kind of intensive sports I'd played to have such damaged shoulders.

A general contractor by trade, John was the one who fixed things around the house. After John died, I knew I would need to fix certain things around the home, and I set out to learn simple tasks. These were the days before the internet, so I bought a copy of *Reader's Digest: Complete Do It Yourself Manual*.

One day I flipped the switch to use the garbage disposal. Nothing happened. I picked up my book and set out to see if I could fix the disposal. Nothing in the book helped me do that, so I went to the home improvement store to purchase a new one.

As I looked at various models, a salesman approached me. "Can I help you choose a garbage disposal?" He then began to explain the features of each model.

As one who knew nothing about choosing a garbage disposal and have always been reluctant to admit what I don't know, I pretended I knew what he was talking about.

Batch feed. Continuous feed. Models from 1/3 to 1 horsepower. Permanent magnetic motor.

Huh?

Trying to portray confidence in my skills and knowledge, I explained to the salesman what my current disposal looked like. "It's black and has two gray hoses coming out of it."

I could see the look on his face. He realized he was dealing with someone with zero knowledge of garbage disposals. He suggested a model he said was "very popular" with customers. I'm guessing he chose the model that was easiest to install. I didn't ask; I just bought the appliance.

I looked at the instructions when I got home with the new garbage disposal. Then, I brought out my Reader's Digest book. The book walked me through the removal of the old garbage disposal. Wow. What a feeling of accomplishment!

Then came the hard part – installing the new one. I didn't realize how heavy that thing was! I had to hold it up with one hand while attaching it to the underside of the sink. All that while I was lying on my back on my kitchen floor with the upper half of my body squeezed into the space under my sink.

I tried several techniques for holding the disposal, but none of them worked. So, I took a break after each try and had a good cry.

I even raged at John for not being there to do this task.

Finally, I got the disposal installed. Holding my breath, I flipped the switch. It worked! It didn't leak! The feeling of exhilaration was terrific. I had to tell someone what I'd done.

I called my friend, Shawn. Tripping over my words and trying to hold back my tears, I told him I had changed out my garbage disposal. He congratulated me. He put down the phone, so he could applaud.

It's been 25 years since I installed that garbage disposal. To this day, every time I see Shawn, he reminds me, and we have a good laugh. But, in private, the memory still makes me cry. It was the first time I'd done something I thought was so difficult at the time. The experience of changing the garbage disposal was my first realization that I could do just about anything.

Chapter 10:

Spider Killer

"Each of us must confront our own fears, must come face to face with them. How we handle our fears will determine where we go with the rest of our lives. To experience adventure or to be limited by the fear of it."

-Judy Blume

I've always been afraid of bugs. Even the smallest of insects make me jump. So, during my marriage to John, whenever I found a bug in the house, I would call for him, and he would take care of the situation. Translation – he would kill the bug and flush it down the toilet.

I remember one time there was a bee in the room. John tried to trap it with a tissue, and the bee stung his finger. That only confirmed my fear of bugs.

One night, about three months after John died, I was up late, smoothing out the plaster on the walls in my bedroom. The kids were asleep, and the house was quiet.

I opened the closet door, and there it was. A spider. I'm terrified of spiders.

Without a thought, I ran toward the stairs to find John, my spider killer. I was halfway down the stairs when I remembered he was gone. So that left just me... and that spider.

I grabbed a box of tissues and returned to that closet. Though shaking, I took the tissue box and killed that spider. After flushing the spider down the toilet, I sat on my floor for a while until the shaking subsided.

That was the day I became the spider killer.

My children have grown up believing I am the fearless warrior who will come as soon as they call when they find a bug is in the house. I will trap and kill any insect, large or small. My kids think I am a force for any insect to reckon with. What they don't know is that, to this day, bugs terrify me.

Chapter 11:

Guilt Sometimes Leads to Bad Decisions

"You spend so much time, so much effort, trying to hold yourself together. And then everything falls apart anyway."

- David Levithan

In the late 1990s, the internet was the craze. I have always been a fan of science fiction and joined an online group of people who wrote amateur scripts for Star Trek shows. Let's say that this was a group that was not afraid to let our geek flags fly.

Dylan was spending time in the fan group, and we began chatting. Back then, people who began a relationship after meeting online were an anomaly. Dylan lived in the Midwest, and I was in Seattle when we began our long-distance relationship via the internet, email, and telephone.

Eventually, Dylan moved to the west coast and in with my kids and me. A year later, we decided to get married. When we married, I asked Dylan if he was okay with not having any other children – I felt that my two kids were enough for me. He agreed, and we married.

A few years into our marriage, Dylan suggested we might be happier if we added a baby to our family. I remember thinking, "This might be a good idea." I love babies, and my two older kids were 6- and 8-years old. I became pregnant with my middle son in December 1998. Dylan and I were both thrilled.

I spent that pregnancy feeling fantastic health-wise. We found out we were having a boy and had several conversations about what we would name him. I made several quilts for my baby. We bought a gorgeous carved oak crib, and I decorated the nursery with many handmade fabric creations.

In the summer of 1999, my friend Dana and I attended a fabric dyeing workshop. The fabrics were tie dyed. I was pregnant, so the instructor asked Dana to be the one to take my fabrics in and out of the chemicals.

I remember the smell of those chemicals. I went home with six different dyed fabrics when the class was over. The plan was to use the fabrics to make a quilt for my son. I made pinwheel shapes with those fabrics and combined them with solid squares. I added that quilt to a stack of other quilts, including a red and white one that had the letters of the alphabet appliqued on it and a wild animal-themed one. The animal one hung on the wall above the changing table. I still have the red alphabet quilt. I also made a carousel horse quilt for my son. I used scrap fabrics and randomly placed the horses on the quilt top. Of all the quilts I made for my son, the carousel horse one was my favorite. I suppose that is why I buried it with him.

My due date was at the end of August 1999. When I went a week past my due date, my labor was induced. I didn't know at the time that the induction drug was not FDA-approved for that purpose. The drug was known to cause intense, lengthy contractions, during which the baby would not receive oxygen. After several hours of labor, it became obvious that my baby was distressed.

Chapter 12:

Ian

"Let go of your expectations. The universe will do what it will. Sometimes your dreams will come true. Sometimes they won't. Sometimes when you let go of a broken dream, another one gently takes its place. Be aware of what is, not what you would like to be, taking place."

-Melody Beattie

On September 4, 1999, my son was born gray and lifeless. He had no heartbeat, and he was not breathing. He was eventually resuscitated and transported to the Neonatal Intensive Care Unit at Children's Hospital in Seattle. I tore a blood vessel during the delivery and could not go to the hospital with the baby. We needed to quickly agree on a name, so we named our son Ian Riley Malone. Dylan went with Ian and the paramedics, and I remember telling him, "Don't leave his side." When Dylan got to the hospital, Ian was whisked away into the emergency room. Dylan was pulled aside to meet with a clerk who wanted to collect the patient's information. Dylan told the clerk, "We need to do this later; I can't leave my son's side." The clerk refused, and security was called. Dylan provided Ian's information, including our insurance information, then he was allowed to go to our son. For years, Dylan would rant about the clerk, whom he referred to as "the twit," anytime he was reminded of the events of that morning.

When I got to the hospital to see Ian later that day, he was connected to a breathing machine. A nurse had to help me get situated to hold my baby with all the tubes, monitors, and IVs he was tethered to. The tears flowed as I held my son in my arms for the first time. I loved him so much.

Children's Hospital of Seattle offered small rooms for parents with children in the Neonatal Intensive Care Unit (NICU). By small rooms, I mean they were rooms measuring about 6' x 8'. There was enough room for a very small bed (about half the size of a twin bed). Dylan and I were given one of those rooms for the first night after Ian was born. We didn't have a change of clothes, toothbrush, or anything other than the clothes we wore when we arrived at the hospital. I didn't sleep that night. I cried until I had no more tears. Dylan and I were never super affectionate toward one another. Growing up in a family where touch is not good, I recoil from hugs or even holding hands. That night, however, Dylan held me while I sobbed. There were no words; there was nothing to say.

When a new baby is born, it is customary to send flowers, cards, or gifts to the family. When Ian was born, we received flowers, but the accompanying cards were more like sympathy cards than congratulations. When I mentioned that to one of my close friends, she began to cry and asked me, "What can we do to support you?" Most people don't have to face that – a friend or loved one experiencing such an awful event. Many of my friends tried to comfort me, but there really wasn't anything helpful a person could say. The best support for me in those days when Ian was in the hospital included the offers to clean my house, take my older kids to and from school, and provide meals. It was the everyday stuff that is most helpful.

In the days after my son was born, the physicians at the hospital were unable to figure out why he wasn't improving. The birth record showed that Ian had normal heart tones up until birth. Expecting to cherish the moment, Dylan videotaped our son's birth. Once it was clear that Ian's medical condition did not match the birth record, Dylan sat down to watch the birth video. He discovered that the providers didn't hear any heart tones from Ian for 20 minutes before his birth. Ian's birth record was falsified by the delivery team.

Before knowing the truth about his birth, the doctors at Children's Hospital told Dylan and me that our baby might have some motor delays, maybe a case of cerebral palsy. One doctor told us, "He may not be an Olympic champion, but he might be a chess champion." So Dylan and I spent time thinking about how we might alter our home to give Ian access, assuming he would have some motor delays.

Before knowing the truth about Ian's injuries, Dylan and I supported using medicines and machines to keep our son alive. We were under the impression that we just needed to get him over this initial hump, and then he would be a child with "some motor delays," but he could also be that "chess champion."

During those early days, Ian was resuscitated numerous times when his heart would stop beating, or he would stop breathing. The nurses would tell us that he was like a bird, and his soul would start to fly away until they would work to bring him back. I was present during several of these events and would rub Ian's chest when he started to fly away. I repeatedly whispered in his ear, "Ian, breathing is fundamental." I would hold him, rocking in my chair. I sang songs to him, and I told him I loved him. I begged him to stay.

During those months while Ian was in the hospital, his true condition became clear. His physicians seemed uncomfortable telling us about the full prognosis for Ian. I remember one physician telling us that we couldn't handle the entire picture. During this time, Dylan and I continued hoping that Ian would survive. Each day, as we learned new, awful details of Ian's injuries, we would lower the bar that was our hopes and expectations. What once seemed black and white suddenly became various shades of gray.

One day while Ian was in the hospital, my husband found me in Ian's room. I was in the fetal position on the floor holding a pooh bear toy and sobbing uncontrollably. Dylan convinced me to visit my doctor to discuss treatment for depression. I remember my doctor thanking

Dylan for arranging that visit. My doctor asked me how I was feeling. I said, "This is a very dark time." What I didn't admit was that I'd considered several possibilities for how I would kill myself to end my pain. Whenever I thought I had a plan, I would remember my two oldest children. There was no plan I could think of that didn't further damage my children. Those two are why I am alive today.

As it became clear that Ian's injuries were far worse than first suspected, Dylan and I sought a consultation with one of Ian's neonatologists. On our next visit, we had a tough conversation.

"Would his condition make sense if I told you he was deprived of oxygen for over 20 minutes prior to birth?" Dylan asked the doctor. The doctor dropped his gaze and answered, "That would make perfect sense. Ian's condition is far too severe to mesh with the information written in his birth record."

His voice cracking, Dylan asked, "With that knowledge, do you believe he has any chance of survival?"

"It is not likely he will survive for long. It depends on how much treatment you choose to give him to keep him alive," said the doctor. Having been silent during the conversation up to this point, I felt as if time was standing still. I asked, "Doctor, are you saying it would be best to let him die?"

"I'm saying it is okay for you to let him die," answered the doctor. Dylan and I used to refer to that doctor as Dr. Kevorkian because he was brutally honest about Ian's condition. That doctor was one of only two physicians in Ian's life who permitted Dylan and me to let Ian go. I've worked in the field of healthcare all my adult life. I know that healthcare professionals want to fix their patients. However, I've found that not many providers are comfortable once they realize they cannot fix their patients. It's as if the provider has their medical bag, and they keep pulling out the tools they have at their disposal. Once there are no more tools, the provider is outside their comfort zone. Unfortunately, this resulted in many providers wanting to provide some kind of care throughout Ian's life, even if that care didn't offer any meaningful purpose.

After several tests and scans, the doctors told us that Ian's outlook was dire. He was not expected to survive long. After consultation with his care team, Dylan and I decided not to resuscitate Ian the next time his little soul tried to fly away. As of that day, Ian no longer had his episodes of stopping breathing or his heart-stopping. He had stabilized.

I was angry at the delivery team for many years for falsifying Ian's birth record. I thought of the hundreds of times Ian was revived and felt that the delivery team had sentenced my son to a miserable life.

For the first month of Ian's life, he was fed through a nasal tube. Ian could not suck nor swallow and had no gag reflex. Any food would likely be inhaled into his lungs, causing aspiration pneumonia. Because he could not protect his airway, he couldn't be fed into his stomach. His nasal feeding tube was weighted so that it passed into the upper intestines. This kept the food and medications from pooling into his stomach, which could be inhaled if he vomited. The nasal tube was taped to the right side of Ian's face, and after a couple of weeks, the right nostril had a larger opening than the left. His beautiful face was becoming distorted.

After two months at Children's Hospital, Ian's condition stabilized. However, his care team still thought he would die at any time, especially once Dylan and I agreed we did not want him resuscitated. We were tired of being in the hospital and wanted to bring our son home.

Our health insurance policy provided for home nursing care, so we knew we could care for Ian at home.

All the NICU nurses at Seattle Children's Hospital were amazing, but we also encountered nurses and physicians in other hospital areas during Ian's stay. One day prior to Ian's discharge from the hospital, a nurse came to see Dylan and me to explain the feeding tube that would be surgically implanted into Ian. Due to the need to provide all nutrition and medication via a surgically implanted feeding tube, Ian needed to undergo surgery. That nurse's name was Jay. She worked with Interventional Radiology. Jay brought the feeding tube to Ian's room and showed it to Dylan and me. She showed us how and where it would be implanted into Ian's abdomen. She explained that the tube needed to be implanted under interventional radiology so the physician could be sure it was properly placed. Jay explained how we would connect Ian's feeding bags, administer the liquid medications, and flush the tube. I was terrified of that tube; though it had a balloon on the end inside Ian to keep it from being dislodged, and there was tape on the abdomen side to keep the tube in place, I knew it could become dislodged. That happened twice during Ian's life, and each time, we needed to go back to the hospital to replace it in the Interventional Radiology department. Jay was there each time. She also came to Ian's funeral years later.

Because Ian required frequent suctioning of his airway, nursing care was needed. Finally, after a mountain of paperwork and home services in place, we brought Ian home.

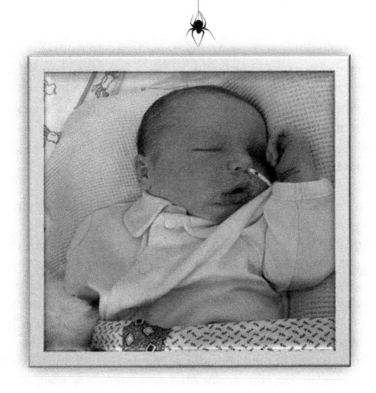

Ian in the NICU at Children's Hospital in Seattle

We all thought it was only a matter of days before Ian would die. After a month at home with nursing care, our insurance company tried to remove coverage for in-home nurses. The insurance company claimed that the nursing care was not medically needed and would not be paid for beyond one month.

Dylan and I tried to reason with our insurance company. Ian's pediatrician wrote letters and called the insurance company. Ian's neurologist did the same. Still, the insurance company remained steadfast in its drive to remove home nursing care. Knowing that media coverage can successfully draw the public eye to an injustice, our attorney arranged for a local media team to interview us at our home. It was our first of many television interviews, and it was the only one where I cried on camera.

The media coverage seemed to work, and our insurance company granted another 30 days of home nursing care for Ian. Within a couple of weeks, when the public eye was no longer upon us, the insurance company sent a letter stating that nursing care was classified as "custodial" and would no longer be covered. We had two more weeks of care before it would be canceled.

I called our insurance company's case manager. Her office was in Atlanta, and she spoke with a southern accent. I asked her what she expected us to do; how would we care for Ian at home without the needed nursing care? The case manager suggested I find local volunteers at my church or college kids to come by if I needed to go to work. I explained that Ian needed tube feeding, numerous medications, and his airway suctioned numerous times per day. These were not tasks that could be performed by a volunteer from my church. "Perhaps you should consider giving up custody to the state. That way, he will be covered under Medicaid," she answered.

In February 2000, the presidential primaries were in full swing. Bill Bradley and Al Gore were coming to our town, and Dylan set out to meet with one of them. Though he went to a rally for Bill Bradley, Dylan was unsuccessful in getting Mr. Bradley to meet with him. After several telephone calls to the Gore campaign, Dylan and I were granted a visit with Al Gore in his hotel room in Seattle.

We packed Ian, his nurse, and Ian's medical equipment and drove to Seattle. After sitting in the hotel lobby for a short while, Al Gore's campaign manager, Donna Brazille, came down to get us. She and the Secret Service agents took us up to Mr. Gore's hotel room. Al Gore answered the door to the room and invited us in. We spent the next half hour telling the presidential candidate our story. At the end of the meeting, Mr. Gore invited us to attend a rally he was attending later that afternoon. We agreed – media coverage helped us once before – maybe we would get another extension of the needed care.

The rally was at a high school in south Seattle. It was well-attended, and Al Gore was late to arrive. Dylan, Ian, the nurse, and I were in the crowd when Al Gore took to the stage and began the rally. He started talking about the need for a Patients' Bill of Rights. Then he told our story. He pointed us out and we were immediately swarmed by the media in the room. After giving several statements, we gave out our contact information and left the rally.

On the drive home from Seattle, we received numerous telephone calls from local television and newspaper media. We set up several interviews to be held in our home that afternoon. I don't remember how many interviews we did that day. We got a call from a producer with The Today Show late in the day. They wanted to interview us on the national program the following morning.

The next morning, a car arrived to take Dylan, Ian, and me to Seattle. It was about 3 am our time. We were taken to the Seattle location for ABC news and interviewed. It was awkward – we couldn't see the faces of Matt Lauer and Katie Couric as they interviewed us; we were facing a screen that showed only our reflection. We didn't realize it, but The Today Show had also arranged for the CEO of our insurance company to be interviewed with us as well. The CEO called into the show and said he had no idea his company was attempting to cut off Ian's needed care. He claimed it was all a mistake and that they weren't planning on cutting Ian's nursing coverage. Seizing the moment, Dylan asked, "Are you saying you won't change Ian's medical care needs unless it is in concert with his treating physician?" The CEO answered yes.

When we got home from that interview, it was still very early. It took a couple of hours, but then the phone calls began. So many requests for interviews, and local politicians called to congratulate us. Some politicians saw our story as a way to further their political goals. We were asked to attend political fundraisers and be photographed for political brochures.

As Al Gore's presidential campaign went on, I was asked to film a commercial for the campaign. The commercial was filmed in my living room, and I was asked to tell my story about how Al Gore saved Ian's insurance coverage. I flubbed one of my lines, but the producers left it in. I think it gave them a more honest look at the commercial. That, and the tears in my eyes. The commercial ran extensively during the campaign. It was titled "Ian," it is 32 seconds in length.

You can view the commercial here:
http://www.livingroomcandidate.org/commercials/2000/ian.

After filming the Ian commercial for Gore's campaign, I became a local celebrity. There were several occasions when I would be told I looked just like that woman in the Gore campaign commercial. As a woman who does not like to be in the limelight, I usually answered, "Yes, I hear that all the time." It was my way of not admitting it was me.

To my friend Ian Malone, with all the best wishes in the world; God Bless You, Al Gore

Ian with Al Gore

Chapter 13:

Settling into Our New Life

"When we allow ourselves to adapt to different situations, life is easier."

-Catherine Pulsifer

As with any case of medical malpractice, Dylan and I retained attorneys. First – we wanted answers. How did all this happen? How could this be prevented so that no other family would experience these events? Because we had the birth video, which clearly showed Ian's birth record was falsified, we had the proverbial "smoking gun." We easily found a legal firm to take our case. Though our case seemed open and shut, we still had to go through the motions. We had depositions, for example. I sat through Dylan's deposition. He faltered and became flustered with the questions from opposing counsel. I started to cry and remembered our attorney sliding the box of tissues toward me.

These depositions are a play on emotions. They are a ploy to bring people down, to wear them down, to cause them to break. The presence of two attorneys (at least), the court reporter, and the providers who caused my son's injuries was intimidating. It made me physically ill to sit through Dylan's deposition. Next, it was my turn.

The providers that caused Ian's injuries were in the room, and they made a point of staring at me through my deposition. I refused to make eye contact. Their attorney questioned me on many things unrelated to Ian's birth and injuries. I was asked about my sex life. I was asked about the births of my two older children. I was asked about the arterial tear I experienced during Ian's birth and if that was why I chose not to accompany my son to Children's Hospital. As if that was a choice. The deposition was exhausting. I was humiliated, and all I could think of was that I had to do this for Ian. Securing funds would help us care for him.

After Dylan and I were deposed, it was time for the two midwives who delivered Ian to have their depositions taken. Our attorney wanted Dylan and I to attend those depositions because of the same intimidation techniques the midwives' attorney played by having them present during Dylan's and my deposition. There was no way I could attend those depositions. My attorney tried to persuade me; he asked Dylan to persuade me. The attorney said it would be more likely the midwives would be truthful if they had to face me. I was not convinced. I did not attend their depositions.

Shortly after the depositions, the providers that caused Ian's injuries offered a full policy settlement. This meant their insurance company would pay the full $2 million policy limits. By offering to settle, the providers would protect themselves from the possibility of a legal verdict that was MORE than their policy maximums, which would result in their financial devastation. However, the providers had one stipulation – they wanted something called a summary judgment. This was a legal statement that they (and we) agreed that these providers were not responsible for Ian's injuries, but the legal documents could find them guilty, so they would agree to pay the full policy limits.

I am a person of principle. I can forgive, and I can move on. But I could not sign a document that said I agreed these providers were not responsible for Ian's injuries. I called my attorney and told him, "I won't sign anything unless you make that summary judgment go away." He was shocked. He said, "We will be getting the full $2 million dollars. You need to sign the summary judgment." I said, "There are times when a person needs to stop submitting to pain. I have suffered enough. Either the summary judgment goes away, or we don't settle." My attorney tried to get Dylan to reason with me. That was to no avail. The provider's attorney withdrew the summary judgment the next day, and we proceeded toward settlement. Part of the settlement was to repay our insurance company for all their expenses. This took nearly all the settlement. The rest was used for care during the years of Ian's life. Even with health insurance, Ian's copays for medical care and medications were over $1000 per month out of our pockets.

Once the battle for nursing coverage was over, we started to settle into our new life. Ian had 16 hours of nursing coverage every day. We arranged for nurses to be in our home from 7am to 11pm. This allowed me to go to work, knowing Ian was in good hands. Dylan's job provided our health insurance coverage, so it was not an option for him to quit working. I moved from working full time to a more flexible schedule so that I could take Ian to his frequent medical appointments. Dylan and I took turns from 11pm to 7am, getting up to tend to Ian's needs throughout the night.

Ian's daily care consisted of connection to his feeding tube for twenty hours daily. His feeding pump could only go at a rate that Ian's digestive system could handle, so it took that many hours to get a full day's calories. That left four hours each day when Ian could be more mobile. During that time, he would be given a bath or taken for a walk in his stroller if he was feeling well enough. Ian's medication regimen was lengthy. He was given medications for his constant seizures, anti-reflux, and more. Ian's medications had to be liquid to be administered through his feeding tube. Ian required surgery every six months to replace his feeding tube. Physical, speech and occupational therapy services were provided in our home.

We had to adapt to having a nurse in our home 16 hours a day. When Dylan and I needed to argue, we would go downstairs to the laundry room to argue outside the nurse's hearing range. The trauma we'd been through and the life we were experiencing at that time took a grave toll on my marriage. Both Dylan and I blamed each other, in part, for what happened to Ian. From Dylan's perspective, my choice of a midwife-assisted birth caused him to blame me. I remember crying out and begging my healthcare providers to stop my labor and transport me for an emergency c-section during my labor with Ian. Though two midwives, two assistant coaches (called doulas), and my husband were in the room, none of them listened to me. Dylan told me he didn't feel he had any power because he wasn't a trained healthcare provider. From my perspective, I couldn't think of an excuse for anyone in the room with me that morning.

Everything in my life was shaken. There was life before Ian's birth and life after – nothing was the same.

Once we were settled into our new life, I filed complaints against the providers who caused Ian's injuries. That included two midwives and the medical doctor who prescribed the labor-induction drug. The Department of Health was provided with all details, including a copy of Ian's birth video. I discovered another patient treated by the same midwives lost her unborn baby due to untreated health conditions. And the doctor? He had multiple complaints against him and had already lost privileges at several hospitals. I thought, for sure, all three providers would either lose their licenses or, at the very least, be suspended. That's not what happened, though. The doctor was told he could no longer prescribe medications for midwifery patients. The two midwives were each ordered to pay a fine of $3000 (payable over three years) and 3 years of probation. Probation consisted of the midwives needing to submit the records of any laboring patient transferred to the hospital. Slaps on the wrist and no assurance that what happened to my son wouldn't happen again. The physician claimed he did not have malpractice insurance, filed for bankruptcy, and moved to Canada.

Some of Ian's nurses were better than others. One nurse was the most caring person I've ever met. One nurse was all about procedure; she caught a fatal medication prescription before it got to Ian. One nurse was caught in several lies and deceptions, including taking some of Ian's medications home with her.

We had our home nurse with us when we took Ian to doctor's appointments. When the media came for interviews, we would ask the nurse if they wanted to be on camera. Each time we would get a new nurse, I would sit with them and discuss our care choices for Ian. We did not intend to resuscitate Ian should he stop breathing. Ian was an incredibly beautiful child, and to look at him, one might not immediately see how damaged he was. We had a few nurses' express hesitation in supporting our care choices. Those nurses were excused.

Dylan and I agreed that our care choices for Ian would focus on keeping Ian comfortable. This meant there were care options we did not choose for Ian, even if those choices made things easier for the care providers. We were incredibly fortunate in the pediatrician we chose to care for Ian. Dr. Katherine Runyon was one of Ian's care team's most caring and compassionate members. Dr. Runyon was the second of two providers during Ian's life who supported our care choices and gave us permission to allow Ian to die.

One day, Ian's home nurse came to Dylan and me to say she was worried about Ian's breathing; she was certain Ian had pneumonia. Dylan and I took Ian to the emergency room and Ian was admitted with a diagnosis of pneumonia. He was placed on oxygen and antibiotics and was in the hospital for a few days. Upon discharge from the hospital, we took Ian to see his pediatrician. Dr. Runyon sat down with us, and she explained, "Ian is going to suffer multiple bouts of pneumonia before he dies. If you keep treating him each time he has pneumonia, you ensure he will suffer more episodes. Do you understand?" One thing about the U.S. healthcare system – they are all about the treatment and how to fix the patient. The truth is, there was no way to fix Ian. Dr. Runyon brought reality to light for us, as hard as it was for us to comprehend. We knew we did not want to sentence him to more suffering than he had to endure.

Years later, when we had another child, we named our daughter Molly Katherine in honor of that amazing pediatrician who supported us and took such great care of Ian.

Though Dr. Runyon was an amazing pediatrician and constant support to Dylan and me, not all doctors were helpful. Once, when Dr. Runyon was unavailable, we took Ian to see another pediatrician in the same office. Ian had pneumonia symptoms, and a chest x-ray confirmed that diagnosis. The pediatrician told us she would arrange for Ian to be admitted to the hospital for IV antibiotics to treat his condition. Ian, his home nurse, and I were in the exam room when the pediatrician gave us her plan. I paused, then explained, "My husband and I have a DNR order for Ian. If you read through Dr. Runyon's notes, you will see our care choices. What I need from you is an order for home oxygen so we can keep him comfortable." That pediatrician just stared at me. Her eyes filled with tears. I had to comfort that doctor, even though I was the patient's mother. Dylan and I decided that we would take Ian to Children's Hospital if Dr. Runyon was unavailable in the future. I didn't ever want to be placed in the position of having to console a doctor due to our care choices for Ian.

There was one bedroom on the main floor of our house. I used that room as my sewing room at the time of Ian's birth. We moved him into the main floor room to avoid having to take Ian upstairs to his original bedroom. This made it much easier to move him in his wheelchair from his room to the kitchen for medications and to the bathroom for baths. I decorated Ian's room with a jungle theme, with wall quilts and curtains, wooden figurines, and posters. We obtained a hospital crib to elevate the head of the bed, which assisted Ian's breathing. We had a kite in the shape of a zebra that hung over his crib, something for Ian to look at as he fell asleep.

Once Ian was given a DNR order, we were referred to Hospice. This included being assigned a Hospice case manager. We were also referred to a Hospice program for siblings. This was a great program, and my two older kids were invited to camping events with other kids who also had a sibling with a life-limiting condition. This was especially important because my older kids were also suffering. I realized my kids weren't getting the attention they needed and deserved and am very thankful for the friends that stepped in to help my family during that time.

Our Hospice nurse put in place several protocols to make our lives easier. First was a protocol for admitting Ian to the hospital. We had standing orders for admission in the event we felt we were unable to care for Ian at home and needed to have him in the hospital. This would keep us from having to go through the Emergency Room. Second, we had orders from Ian's pediatrician to administer morphine for "air hunger." This meant that when Ian was struggling to breathe, we would administer liquid morphine, which would slow down his breathing and thereby lessen his body's hunger for air. At the end of his life, Ian's dosage of morphine was rising due to him becoming more tolerant of the drug, and we had some nurses who worried about giving him a higher dose. I remember one night when Ian was struggling to breathe, his nurse did not want to provide a higher dose, so I called our Hospice nurse. I remember the calm voice on the other end of the line as the nurse said to me, "Christine, if he is still struggling to breathe, you have not given him enough. You are not ending his life by medicating him; you are making him more comfortable."

Each night, our family cat would sleep next to Ian. I've heard that pets are very comforting, which was true with Ian. With the mental age of about a two-month-old, Ian didn't understand the cat. I'm not sure Ian recognized his parents, but I'd like to think he did. But when the cat slept with him, Ian's oxygen levels were higher, and his heart rate was more regular.

Dylan and I were referred to a facility not far from our home that offered respite care for very sick children. We could take Ian to that facility for week-long stays 3 or 4 times per year. It was during those times when Dylan and I would plan a family vacation with our other children, or just stay home without having alarms to tend to at night.

Caring for Ian was no small task. He would typically be sleeping when his nurse would arrive at 7 am. The nurse would work for eight hours and then be relieved by the second nurse of the day. The second nurse would care for Ian from 3-11 pm. There were days when the nursing agency was unable to provide nursing care. This included all holidays. When this happened, it would typically be me that would stay home to care for Ian while Dylan went to work.

Taking Ian in for medical appointments was no small task. For the first year of Ian's life, we transported him in his car seat, specially modified to support his airway. At about age one, Ian got his first wheelchair. It was bright blue with glitter in the fabric. The wheelchair was specially fitted for Ian with a headrest, a strap to hold his head back, so his airway was open, several straps and molded areas to hold him in place, and straps to keep his feet in their holders. That first chair even had a shade that could be attached. Ian looked like a little prince in that chair.

Once we had the wheelchair, we still transported Ian in his special car seat, with the wheelchair folded and placed in the trunk. When we got to our destination, I would get the wheelchair out, get Ian into his wheelchair, and off to the medical appointment we would go.

We had a handicapped parking permit. One day, I was taking Ian to a medical appointment, and I parked in a handicapped space and got out of the car. A woman getting out of a nearby car began to lecture me about parking in a handicapped spot. She clearly saw that I didn't have any visual disabilities. I ignored her, which made her even more vocal and angry. I went to the trunk of my car and removed the wheelchair. As I set up the chair and began to get Ian out of his car seat and into the chair, the woman stopped yelling at me. I looked up at her and said, "Is there anything else you would like to say?" She mumbled an apology and quickly moved away.

One thing I learned in my years with Ian was that there isn't much I can't do. I took my son for visits with Santa, for example, along with my older children. I remember one trip to visit Santa; there were several steps from the floor to the platform where Santa sat. There was no wheelchair ramp. I've always been vocal about accessibility for persons with disabilities, and, during Ian's life, this was certainly the case. I mentioned to Santa's team that they were not accessible to all children by having those steps to get to Santa. They stood there with blank faces. Then Santa got up from his chair, climbed down the stairs, and squatted next to Ian. He told the photographer to take photos as they improvised the scenery. Santa insisted that his team not charge me for those photos. The next year, when I took the kids to the same location to see Santa, there was a ramp. It is stories such as these that help me see the silver lining of Ian's life. Helping others, even though he had no concept of what was happening around him.

When we did not have nursing care, there were events that Dylan and I could not attend as a family. One of us would need to be home. Dylan and I would choose – which one of us would go to a family wedding, see one of our kids sing in the choir, or attend our kids' school graduations.

There are many things I used to take for granted before Ian came into my life. As I think back on some of those things, I sometimes feel ashamed. Selfish. I remember when my oldest son was an infant, he spit up all over my blazer just before I was leaving for work. I was in such a tizzy over that blazer. After Ian, something like spitting up on a blazer was as meaningless to me as losing a sock in the dryer.

When my oldest son was in high school, he had a good friend named Jesse. This friend suffered from a seizure disorder and his mother wasn't comfortable letting Jesse stay overnight at my home, in case he had a seizure. I assured her that Jesse would be okay and, one weekend, she agreed that Jesse could spend the night. She warned us that Jesse's seizures worsened late into the evening, so he should be in bed no later than 10pm. Being high school boys, my son and his friend ignored that warning. It was about midnight when I heard a loud BANG from the kitchen. When I got to the kitchen, I saw Jesse in a grand mal seizure on the kitchen floor. I calmly got a bath towel to place under his head so he would not hit his head against the wood floor. I rolled Jesse to his side, and I asked my son to call his mother. Jesse's mother told us she would be right over and not to call 9-1-1. Jesse's seizure lasted about a minute. When he came to, he asked for a drink of water. I wasn't sure if he should have anything, even water, just after a seizure, so I told him his mother was on her way. When Jesse's mother arrived, I think she expected us to be frantic. After all, how many people have watched a person in a grand mal seizure? Instead, I calmly described the events, including that I would not give him water. I remember that mom staring at us as if we were some sort of aliens. She had no idea. Ian sometimes had over 200 seizures in a day. What was one measly seizure to us? From that day on, Jesse's mother allowed him to stay overnight at my house whenever the teens wanted to get together.

During Ian's life, there were many times when I would injure my back. Though I know how to safely lift a heavy item, lifting and carrying Ian was not as simple as lifting a box. After lifting Ian to place him in his chair, or the bath, he would sometimes lurch his body, causing the person carrying him to lurch as well, to keep from dropping him. I learned to live with constant back pain, frequently used a Velcro back brace, and made frequent visits to my doctor for a few days of medications when flare-ups would occur.

It was during one of these flare-ups that Dylan and I were invited to film a commercial advocating for a Patients' Bill of Rights in Washington state. I was asked to bring several clothing items so the producers could choose what they thought was the right look for me. They went with a gold button-up sweater. No jewelry. I looked very matronly. I was given my lines, and filming began. I could tell that the producer was not getting exactly what he wanted. He said to me, "I was hoping we could get a more... pained look on your face." I said okay, and I purposely twisted my back. Yeah, the pain on my face in that commercial was real.

During Ian's life, I developed a keen sense of hearing regarding alarms. Ian had alarms that would go off if his feeding tube malfunctioned, another alarm for his respiration rate, another for his oxygen saturation level, and another for his heart rate. Toward the end of his life, Ian also had constant oxygen. The oxygen machine was one more alarm. To this day, the sound of alarms causes me to tense up; I need to know what the alarm is and why it is going off.

Chapter 14:
Molly Joins Us

"Look closely and you will see.

Almost everyone carrying bags.

Of cement on their shoulders.

That's why it takes courage.

To get out of bed in the morning

And climb into the day."

- Edward Hirsch

Dylan and I wanted to experience a "happy" parenting experience, so I became pregnant again in the spring of 2000. Ian was six months old, and I remember thinking I wouldn't be able to safely lift and care for him if I waited any longer to have another baby.

During my fourth pregnancy, I wanted to do things completely different than I had before. Dylan and I chose to not know the gender of the baby. I didn't buy even one outfit, toy, or diapers for the new baby. My doctor knew of the events that caused Ian's injuries, and I could tell she was intimidated by me. My due date was New Year's Day 2001. We didn't have home nursing care for Ian on holidays, so going into labor on New Year's Day meant I would not have Dylan with me at the hospital.

When we told our two older children that we would have another baby, my daughter asked me, "Where will we put the other nurse?" In her young mind, babies came with nurses.

I went into labor late afternoon on New Year's Day 2001. I called the hospital and spoke to the nurses about when I should come in. They knew of me and didn't want to take any chances, so they told me to come in immediately. Dylan needed to stay home to care for Ian because we wouldn't have a home nurse until the following day at 7 am. So, I drove myself ten blocks to the hospital. It was late at night, and I stopped every few blocks to breathe through contractions. I was the only "single" mother there when I got to the hospital, and I walked the hallways as my labor progressed.

The arrival of our home nurse at 7 am meant Dylan could join me at the hospital. Early in the afternoon of January 2nd, my water broke. Up until that point in time, everything seemed happy, safe, and wonderful. But there was meconium in the fluid. This was an indication that the baby may be in distress. Delivering a child when there is meconium in the fluid brings about a risk that the child may breathe in the substance, causing health issues that could be severe.

I am a strong-willed person. I speak up for myself and don't like it when someone looks to speak for me. But, at that moment, I lost control... my will... my power. All I could think of was that my baby was going to die.

Dylan and my doctor talked about options as if I was not there. It was like I was watching them from outside a window. My doctor brought in additional nurses and a pediatric respiratory therapist in preparation for the birth. They purposefully did not allow the baby to take a breath until completely delivered to avoid any inhalation of that meconium. After being born, the baby was taken to a bassinet near my bed, where nurses, doctors, and respiratory therapists performed their exams. I heard the baby crying. Dylan and I both cried tears of joy. Ten minutes after the birth, one of the nurses asked my doctor, "Do they know they have a girl?" It didn't occur to us to ask; it wasn't important to know. Instead, we wanted to know the baby's APGAR score (a quick test performed on all newborns to determine how well the baby tolerated the birth). The baby was crying, and that was all that mattered. She was pink, she was healthy, and she was our daughter, Molly. On the way home from the hospital, we stopped at the store to buy diapers.

Chapter 15:
Losing a Piece of My Heart

"You will lose someone you can't live without, and your heart will be badly broken, and the bad news is that you never completely get over the loss of your beloved. But this is also the good news. They live forever in your broken heart that doesn't seal back up. And you come through. It's like having 'a broken leg that never heals perfectly—that still hurts when the weather gets cold, but you learn to dance with the limp."

- Anne Lamott

During the last two weeks of Ian's life, his condition deteriorated rapidly. He required constant oxygen with a facial mask to keep his oxygen saturation level at or above 75 (normal is 95+) and he had fevers so high they would max out an analog thermometer at 107 degrees. It was early on a Saturday morning, May 1st, 2004. Dylan and I were asleep when our cat (Data) jumped on our bed. He stood on my chest and began kneading and meowing. This was very unusual for the cat, so I got up. I reached the first floor just as Ian's alarms sounded. He had stopped breathing. By waking me up, the cat gave me the gift of being with my son as he passed away. It was the greatest gift I've ever received.

A few years later, that cat began to lose weight; his vet diagnosed him with liver cancer and, because of his advanced age, recommended we keep loving him until the cat told us it was time to let him go.

The cat spent the rest of his days eating raw tuna, raw salmon – anything he wanted. He loved to sit on the kitchen windowsill, enjoying the afternoon sun. Then, one morning, Data looked at his raw fish and walked away. I knew he was telling me it was time to let him go. My husband offered to take him to the vet, saying, "You don't have to do this. Let me be the one to take the cat to the vet." I knew I needed to be with Data when he crossed that rainbow bridge.

I took Data to the vet, where he was on his favorite blanket (one that once belonged to Ian), purring and drooling. It was over in just a few seconds, and the vet left me alone with Data until I was ready to go. I tried to be quiet, but I knew the sound of my sobs could be heard outside that exam room.

Data Kitter

When I received Data's cremains, I placed his collar and tags around the top of the urn. The urn sits on the kitchen windowsill today, where he can forever enjoy the afternoon sun.

During his life, my family was consumed with the things Ian needed. Our routine was exhausting. The first few days after Ian died, the media came around again. They ran stories about Ian's death and the legacy he left behind. Al Gore called to express his condolences and sent flowers to the funeral – he was out of the country and unable to make it in person.

One thing that was very helpful in having Hospice involved in our case was that we did not need to call 9-1-1 when Ian died. Instead, we called the Hospice nurses, who sent a nurse to our home to verify that Ian had passed. She then called the medical examiner to report Ian's death and obtain a number for the death certificate. The nurse then called the local funeral home. She explained that the funeral staff would come into my home with a gurney to take Ian away. Next, the nurse explained that the funeral staff would have to zip Ian into a bag to transport him. The gentle way the nurse explained all of this to me was very calming. I'm glad I was told he would be zipped into a bag before seeing it done.

Our home had a front and back entrance. The morning Ian died, the Hospice nurse arranged for the funeral home to pick Ian up through the alley entrance, not causing our neighbors to notice. The Hospice nurse arranged for our rented medical equipment to be picked up by the vendors, and she destroyed the remaining liquid morphine we still had in the house.

Dylan and I went to the funeral home and picked a child-size coffin. It was white with a white satin lining. I brought an outfit for Ian to be dressed in. It was a green and white plaid shirt with green pants and suspenders. I brought socks, but no shoes. Ian never liked wearing shoes. I told the funeral home staff that I wanted Ian's feeding tube removed before he was buried. I explained how they would remove it. It was important to me that Ian not be buried with that feeding tube.

I chose a pop-up book that Ian was very fond of and placed that in with Ian. I covered him with the carousel quilt I'd made him years before. Dylan contacted a boys' choir in California. They agreed to come to the funeral to sing. They sang a song titled "Pie Jesu." It was the most beautiful song I've ever heard; those boys sounded like angels. The funeral home was not large, and it was packed. The pastor asked if anyone would like to share memories. Many people did. The most memorable for me was Ian's pediatrician. She cried as she shared that caring for Ian, and working with my family, made her a better physician.

I asked Ian's team of nurses if they would like to be pallbearers. My thought was to acknowledge that they carried Ian throughout his life and would carry him to his final resting place. I wasn't sure if any of those nurses would want to participate. I was surprised that ALL of them wanted to participate, so a team of eight nurses crowded around that small child-size casket and carried Ian from the hearse to the gravesite after his funeral service.

As Ian's casket was lowered into his grave, Dylan played Amazing Grace on his flute.

Dylan and I created a press release to announce Ian's death:

Ian Malone, Gore's Poster Child for the Patients' Bill of Rights, Dies in Everett at Age 4

EVERETT, WA -- Nationally recognized symbol of the need for health care reform, Ian Riley Malone died this morning from complications of his birth injury. Ian was four years old.

Injured by medical errors at the time of his birth, the Malones brought Ian home from the hospital at three months of age with the aid of home nursing care. When Ian's insurance company announced, it was no longer going to provide the care Vice President Gore intervened and restored the lifesaving treatment.

After a successful trip to Olympia to lobby for a Patients' Bill of Rights Ian was given the pen Gov. Locke used to sign the bill. Later featured in national television campaigns aimed at passing a federal version of the bill, Ian became involved in the fight in the Congress to improve health care.

Statement by the Malone family:

"Ian's short life was a constant battle to improve the system for those who will come after him. We will sorely miss his beautiful smile and ready laugh and are sorry his journey had to end so soon."

A memorial service will be held at Purdy Walters and Cassidy on Pacific Avenue in Everett Saturday, May 8th at 1pm.

While Dylan was making arrangements for Ian's funeral services, I wrote the obituary. It was important to me that we acknowledge everyone involved in Ian's care, from the doctors and nurses to the UPS deliveryman who brought us supplies. Each was a vital member of Ian's care team.

Ian Riley Malone, 4, died May 1, 2004, due to complications from injuries sustained at birth.

Born September 4, 1999, in Everett, WA to Dylan and Christine Malone, medical errors deprived Ian of oxygen and he nearly died during birth. After three months in hospitals Ian was discharged with the aid of home nursing care. When Ian's HMO refused to provide the life-saving care, denied all appeals, and suggested that he be put up for adoption, his parents angrily refused.

Ian became a nationally recognized symbol of the need for healthcare reform when Vice President Gore intervened on his behalf and ensured that his healthcare needs would be met for the rest of his life. A close personal bond formed instantly between little Ian and Al and Tipper Gore, and his family takes great comfort in their years of friendship.

Ian loved music, water, and spinning in his wheelchair. His favorite color was yellow, and he took great delight in being read to, or watching people dance. Always ready with a smile, Ian was a happy boy who found pleasure in things many of us took for granted.

A special child, Ian was someone who touched the lives of many people, some of whom he never met. His contribution to the conversation on healthcare reform and the plight of those injured due to medical malpractice resulted in changes in policy on both the local and national level.

Ian leaves behind his mother Christine, father Dylan, brother Corey, sisters Mallory and Molly, grandparents, aunts, uncles, cousins and countless friends – all of whom will miss him dearly.

A special thank you to Katherine Runyon, MD, the nurses and staff of New Care Concepts, the physical and occupational therapists, the staff of Health team NW, the providers and staff Ian visited at CHRMC, the staff of Children's Country Home, Bartell's Pharmacy staff, and our UPS deliveryman. You have all served integral parts on Ian's team and without each of you we couldn't have cared for him at home.

A memorial service open to the public will be held at Purdy & Walters with Cassidy Funeral Home 1702 Pacific Ave, Everett on Saturday, May 8, 2004, at 1:00PM. Interment will be at Cypress Lawn Memorial Park, Everett, WA.

*In lieu of flowers, the family suggests memorials be made to **Providence Hospice and Home Care of Snohomish County, 2731 Wetmore Ave., Suite 500, Everett WA 98201.***

The week after Ian's funeral, our UPS deliveryman knocked on my door. He had tears in his eyes, and he thanked me for acknowledging his part in Ian's care. He told me he never realized how incredibly important a person delivering packages could be.

Chapter 16:
The Aftermath

"Great losses are great lessons."

- Amit Kalantri

I found homes for Ian's medical equipment. Families with children like my Ian, who could not obtain the equipment due to lack of insurance coverage, were happy to receive these items. However, there was one thing I could not give away just yet – Ian's wheelchair.

The nursing agency that supplied us with home nursing care sent us a Golden Chain tree. Ian responded to the color yellow and watching that tree bloom in my yard every year made my heart smile. In addition, the city where we lived donated a bench with a plaque commemorating Ian's life. The bench was installed in the park across the street from our home.

Ian's tree in bloom

When Ian died, I was one year away from finishing my undergraduate college degree. The instructor of one of the classes I was taking invited me to meet her on campus to discuss her department's needs. This instructor was aware of my work in healthcare administration and wanted to know if I would be interested in writing curricula for administrative medical assisting courses. I agreed and proceeded to write the curricula for a series of classes. When they could not find an instructor to teach one of those courses the next quarter, the leadership team asked me if I would be willing to teach a class.

Before Ian was born, I believed in setting long-term goals. I believed that I'd had enough loss and grief in my life. During my pregnancy with Ian, I did what many parents do — I thought of all the lessons I would need to teach my son in his life — lessons designed to help him become a good man. Shortly after Ian was born, I realized the tables were turned. I wouldn't be teaching him — instead, it was Ian who taught me the lessons in life that helped me to become a better person.

Before Ian was born, I measured my success by how much money I was making, how busy I was with work, and what my professional title was. During Ian's life, I found myself being classified as only one thing — a victim of medical malpractice. I remember going to various events and encountering people who were surprised that I was educated and wasn't the quiet mother of a disabled baby.

Though I suffer from severe depression and panic attacks to this day, I am happy to have had Ian in my life. I've learned where my buttons are, and I recognize my limitations. I purposefully avoid situations where I might be triggered. That isn't always easy to do.

When working in a healthcare leadership role, I covered for the manager of the pediatrics department one day. I received a call from a nurse in that department telling me she had an upset parent and could I come over to assist. When I arrived in the department, I found myself faced with a young father. His infant daughter was in a stroller, a feeding tube down her nose and taped to her face. I could tell by her movements that she was severely disabled. The father complained that the nurse would not submit an order for the liquid food his daughter needed because the official policy was for those requests to come in at least 24 hours before needed. I lost my mind. I told the father that the referral would be placed, and he should go to the pharmacy to pick it up. After he left, I turned to the nurse and told her, "I may not be your boss, but I am a boss, and you are going to submit that referral right now." She did. I returned to my desk, shut my office door, and sobbed. That experience validated that I would never work in a pediatric department.

Ian helped me find my voice. My purpose. My life wasn't supposed to be one of success measured by money and titles — it was supposed to be one where I would take my lessons learned and use them to help others.

Chapter 17:

Riley Joins Us

"Do you not know that a man is not dead while his name is still spoken?"

-Terry Pratchett

It was two years after Ian died. My family consisted of two children from my first marriage and my daughter with Dylan. Including Ian, I'd had four children. I felt a bit selfish. I had two healthy daughters and one healthy son. Life was good, and I'd learned so many life lessons. Why have one more baby? The truth is that I was distracted during my pregnancy and early childhood with Molly. Ian, and his care, ruled my life. I wanted one last opportunity to have a "normal" pregnancy and birth. I was 42 years old. What were the chances I could become pregnant again? Alas, it happened.

I became pregnant in March of 2006. I sought care with the same OB/GYN that cared for me and delivered my daughter, Molly. I was clearly one of her oldest patients and I would arrive for my prenatal visits dressed in my business suit, very professional... and the other younger mothers were wearing pajama pants and slippers.

During that pregnancy, due to my advanced age, I had all the genetic testing offered. I discovered that I was having a boy and that he didn't have any of the 400+ genetic anomalies that I was tested for. My baby was healthy. Dylan and I thought about a name. We brought my oldest children into the naming game, and I created index cards with names that Dylan and I liked. We showed those cards to the two older kids, asking them to choose their favorites. One of the names in the running was Rowan. While I was pregnant with my youngest son, I worked on my first textbook with Pearson Publishers. Just before my son's birth, I wrote the dedication. I thanked my children, and I listed my youngest child as "Rowan."

A few weeks before my youngest child's birth, Dylan and I agreed on the name "Riley."

My youngest son was born in 2007, three years after Ian died. I'd already used the name "Riley" with Ian as his middle name... but I also regretted not using that for a child as a first name. We chose the middle name Sean to honor one of my long-time friends.

As I came to the end of my pregnancy, my doctor suggested my labor be induced and have a controlled birth. I agreed and was admitted to the hospital on December 14, 2007, to have my labor induced for my fifth child.

Everything was going along smoothly, then the baby's heart rate dipped after a contraction. The nurses rushed into the room, and I felt myself return to that place during Molly's birth – Dylan and the doctor were talking about me as if I wasn't there. The doctor suggested a c-section, and I quickly agreed. Riley was born a healthy baby. Afterward, my doctor came to me and said, "He was never in any danger."

At my post-op visit, I apologized to the doctor for my anxiety during Riley's birth. She said, "It's not surprising, given your PTSD." It had been eight years since Ian's birth.

Chapter 18:

Teaching as Therapy

A teacher affects eternity; he can never tell where his influence stops.

— Henry B. Adams

I was surprised to find how much I enjoyed teaching. I've never thought of myself as a patient person and didn't believe I had the patience to work with students. What I found, however, was that working with students, teaching them about patient safety and working with patients and their needs, was my life's calling. I would never have known that if not for Ian.

One of the classes I taught for years is an Intercultural Communications in Healthcare class. One of my lectures in that class is on death and grief. I share my own personal stories of loss and grief in that lecture. My goal has always been to help my students better understand loss and grief so that when they go into their future careers in healthcare, they will be better able to help their patients.

Many years ago, a student in my Intercultural Communications class wrote a paper for extra credit. The student was Kirk Gomez and he's given me permission to share his paper in this book.

Pure Emotion by Kirk Gomez

Christine appeared to be another instructor teaching another class I just had to get through. A class for which I had low expectations and after I passed, I would probably not give it a second thought. I underestimated her and the class itself because somewhere, without my knowledge, I was learning new things that pertained to my career and life itself. During class I stopped following along in my book and quit taking notes because I didn't want to miss anything. I learned far more from listening and visualizing lessons and situations than from the traditional note taking and lecture style. This class quickly became my favorite of the quarter and will probably be the most unforgettable class of my stay at EvCC. The way she got everyone to debate and interact in the classroom had your gears constantly turning, but in the most relaxing and entertaining way.

Continuing with peeling back the layers of Christine's experiences, you find hardships that would break most people. She stated her experiences were a deciding factor in getting into teaching. I think those of us who happen to stumble upon this class will be forever thankful for taking not only knowledge, but also life lessons in general.

A complication during labor left a baby without any oxygen for nearly twenty minutes. Stop and try to imagine that. Twenty minutes is an eternity without air! I'm not deeply religious, but the fact he could be brought back I think was proof god had bigger plans for him. His life indirectly impacted mine and others in our class. If you sit back and think about it, would we even have a class like this if he weren't a part of this world? It is pretty inspiring that a four-year-old still lives on touching people to this day. If you google Ian Malone's name, you find both he and his family are heroes in the healthcare system. Like superman, I doubt he would have chosen this life for himself. But it is true, a trip to Olympia with the previous help of Vice President Al Gore, Governor Locke signed a bill that knocked down a few walls for a change in the health care reform. And who do you think got to keep the pen they used to sign the Bill? A brown-haired little angel with rosy cheeks; Ian Malone. From one picture I've seen of Ian, you can almost hear his cute little baby snore. And in another in a wheelchair with a yellow and green toy his eyes and smile were nothing short of honesty and innocence.

It was interesting to find how insurance dropped the ball on this one. If Christine's family and Ian were able to make changes, I wonder what each of us could do. This also tied into my question of how to educate parents who don't use the healthcare system to its full potential. Christine stated she would give parents resources and educate where they could go if they couldn't afford it, or if insurance wouldn't cover it. From the newspaper articles you can see she knows a thing or two about this subject. Again, this is that teaching without knowing you're being taught. Like a wise sensei, we are just young grasshoppers! I now realize the importance of having resources at hand. Because, if we don't start to be the professionals we want in the healthcare system, how do we expect the change we want?

In closing, I am grateful for the opportunity to have taken such a life lesson class. I paused a couple times while writing my paper to just watch my son eat a peanut butter and jelly sandwich and realized how lucky I am. Ian couldn't hold his head up, suck, *swallow, or gag, but he was described by his mom as "pure emotion." So rather than fill this paper with fluff and wasted words, I will take a page out of Ian's book and hope whoever reads this can look at someone they love, or remember a face, and, without words, just experience "pure emotion." Thank you, Ian Malone.*

Over the years, I've had students come back to visit me and tell me a story of how something they learned in one of my classes helped them when they worked with their patients. This is the most satisfying thing I've ever experienced in my professional life.

Patient safety is a passion for me. I saw a story once that the halls of NASA are lined with drawings from the astronauts' children. This is done to remind everyone on the team of the humanity involved, and that those going up in space have families that love them. I try to impress on my healthcare students the same line of thinking. None of us is just a name on a chart, we are all important, we all have value.

Chapter 19:

Interviews and Presentations

"We do not learn from experience... we learn from reflecting on experience."

-John Dewey

Though I'd agreed to several interviews during Ian's life, I only gave one after he died. As an introvert, it really isn't comfortable for me to talk about myself. Giving interviews during Ian's life had a purpose – to keep his insurance coverage for home nursing care in place. Once Ian was gone, that purpose was no longer there, and I stopped accepting interview invitations. Even more than 20 years after his death, I still receive interview requests now and then. I turn them all down.

The only interview I gave after Ian's death was with a local Seattle newspaper. I accepted that interview because I believed the reporter would dive deeper into my family's story. Most people realize that news reports are not always accurate. I can attest to that. Some of the stories published about my family contained small errors, such as misspelling a name. Others contained large errors, such as changing the narrative and the truth.

The story this reporter wrote was the most accurate one ever published about my family. The reporter went into detail about not only what happened to my son but the need for reform of the healthcare system so that the injuries Ian sustained were few and far between. During the meeting, the reporter and I watched Ian's birth video. It was the first and last time I watched that video. The interview lasted nearly five hours, and at the end, both the reporter and I were in tears. I was exhausted and completely spent. No more interviews for me.

I've been invited to give presentations on various healthcare topics over the years, partly due to my years of experience working in healthcare and partly due to my work as an educator. Most of those presentations focus on a particular topic – customer service or patient satisfaction, for example. Occasionally, I give presentations on working with grieving patients. Though I include some personal stories both in my presentations and my classes, I've never gone into detail about how I've felt through any of the tragedies I've endured.

That changed one day when I was asked to give a presentation to a group of healthcare providers. The request was for me to discuss what it feels like to be a victim of medical errors. At first, I thought it would be too difficult to get through such a presentation. Growing up in a dysfunctional environment, I learned it was safest to keep my emotions and feelings to myself.

The presentation was entitled "*The Human Face of Medical Errors.*" My audience was about 30 medical doctors, some of whom I'd met professionally. While some of these providers knew that I'd lost a child to medical errors, none of them knew anything personal about me. In my presentation, I covered my son's injuries briefly. This presentation wasn't about Ian; it was about my family.

It was difficult to put the presentation together. I relived some memories that I hadn't thought about in several years. I exposed my vulnerabilities. I included the time my husband found me on the floor of Ian's room, holding a baby toy, curled into the fetal position, and sobbing. I said, "That was a dark time."

I started that presentation with my professional façade showing. No emotions, just statements. That was, of course, impossible to hold on to. Looking at my audience, I saw tears streaming down their faces. These are medical providers, I remember thinking, and many of them had never thought about the aftermath the patient and their family go through after a medical error.

I explained to these providers how I experience PTSD when I go in for healthcare, especially if it involves care for my children. I overanalyze things; I think of the possible negative outcomes. Sometimes, I cannot make a decision, based on my fears. I call those times "analysis paralysis."

I know that horrible things can happen in healthcare, and I've become jaded in many ways. One of the things I like most about teaching is that I am in a room with students who are not jaded, students who do not know firsthand how awful events can occur, especially when the occasion is supposed to be so wonderful. I've often told my students, "If you were not aware of how important your work is in patient care, you will be at the end of my class."

I know, from my work on patient safety issues, that medical mistakes don't typically happen due to one single event. It is usually a series of events, with multiple people playing a part. In my case with Ian, there were many places where someone involved could have stopped the process and possibly prevented the outcome. From the person who answers the phone to schedule a patient to the surgeon who performs a surgery – we all play a part in patient safety. We need to remember that and the awesome responsibility each role holds.

Chapter 20:

Death Anniversary

"I do not believe that sheer suffering teaches. If suffering alone taught, all the world would be wise since everyone suffers. To suffering must be added mourning, understanding, patience, love, openness, and the willingness to remain vulnerable."

– Anne Morrow Lindbergh

Ian's death anniversary is always a melancholy day for me. On one hand, I am reminded of the son I love - the one I lost - and I am sad. On the other hand, I am reminded of the son I love - the one who is still with me in my heart - and I am happy that he is no longer in pain. That double-edged sword brings both pain and happiness, all in one thrust.

I was talking once with an acquaintance who has also lost a child. She told me she spends the death anniversary doing something to celebrate her child's life. During our conversation, we both acknowledged that how we spend these special days is so very personal.

Where she wants to surround herself with friends and family and celebrate her child... I want solitude and quiet time to reflect upon mine. She is not in denial any more than I am lingering in pain. We just have different methods for channeling our grief. And for channeling our joy.

My son gave me a view of life that I will always hold dear. Yes, it hurts to remember he is gone, but it also feels good to remember him. I know many people shy away from talking to me about Ian, for fear the conversation will make me sad. The truth is, I love to talk about my son.

Some years, the death anniversary is harder than others. Sometimes the death anniversary hits me when other stressors are happening in my life.

Chapter 21:
Changes

"Loss can be even louder during the holiday months and change the lens through which you see and feel everything. Twinkling lights seem as thou they are dimmed somehow. The sparkle has dulled. The music has quieted. The joy, hope, and magic of the season feels out of reach. Grief doesn't take a holiday."

- Liz Newman

After Vince died, I noticed changes in my life. I changed the color of my hair and found there were foods I no longer wanted to eat. After John died, I didn't want to celebrate holidays, but I did so for my children. The first Christmas after John died, I put up the Christmas tree and let the kids decorate it. The decorations were only on the bottom third of the tree. My kids and I developed new traditions and, when Dylan joined the family, we added even more.

Ian's last Christmas was 2003. He was too sick to make a trip out to visit Santa with the other kids. Our local Hospice group heard of this, and Santa and Mrs. Claus visited Ian at home.

Ian with Santa and Mrs. Claus, Christmas morning, 2004

After Ian died, many of those newfound holiday traditions were no longer interesting to me. I didn't want to go to the tree farm as a family and chop down a tree. I didn't want to decorate at all. That first year, we bought an artificial tree because I thought if there was no smell of a Christmas tree, perhaps the holiday would be easier for me. It wasn't. I went through the motions for my kids. Dylan used to take the kids to the store to have them pick out a gift for me. He also used to get me a gift from Ian. That first Christmas after Ian died, Dylan asked me, "Should we continue to give gifts from Ian, now that he has died?" No. That would be far too painful of a reminder for me.

Sometimes, I find myself wanting to write a note to Ian. This often happens around his birthday. This is the note I wrote to him the day before his 15th birthday:

What would it be like?
An open note to my son, Ian...

Tomorrow, September 4th, would be your fifteenth birthday. I can't believe so much time has passed since you were born! Your dad and I were sooo excited to have you join our family. Your older brother, Corey, wanted to name you Skeletor - hey, don't hold it against him - he was six and a big fan of the Masters of the Universe at the time. Oh, how much we planned for your arrival. I painted the nursery a wonderful green color. We bought a carved oak crib and matching dresser. I made you several baby quilts. Everything was so planned, so perfect.

The morning you were born it was a clear day. Not a cloud in the sky. My labor was induced, and everything was supposed to be perfect. You were going to be (and were) my biggest baby (at over 10 pounds!) so I bought lots of three-month-old baby clothes. No newborn stuff for you! We knew you were a boy, but we couldn't agree on a name. I wanted to call you Riley, your dad wanted Ian. We settled on Ian Riley Malone. A strong name. Things went really (really) bad during my labor with you and the people responsible for the safety of both of us really let us down. I am so sorry that happened. When you were born you had already left this earth, but the paramedics brought you back. At such a cost to you. I am so sorry for that.

At first, while you were in the hospital, I prayed for your recovery. Because your birth record had been falsified, the doctors at Children's didn't know the extent of your injuries. It was the birth video that brought the truth to light, but by then you were two months old. For the first two months, you stopped breathing so many times. I remember my mantra to you was, "Ian - breathing is fundamental!" and you would be urged back into this world. I am so sorry I didn't let you go then; I just didn't know how bad your injuries were. Your dad and I were told you might have cerebral palsy, maybe some learning disabilities. When the awful truth was known - that you would never suck nor swallow, that you would never hold up your head or have any purposeful movement, that your life would be one of chronic aspiration pneumonia... well, the decision to let you go during one of your apneic moments was gone. You had stabilized by then. We had inadvertently sentenced you to years of struggling to breathe, constant seizures, and painful medical procedures.

By the time we brought you home from the hospital at 8 weeks of age, it was clear you would not be with *us for long. We wanted to keep you as comfortable as possible, but we did not want to selfishly prolong your life, and thereby prolong your suffering. You hung in there. Such a determined spirit! Every decision your dad and I made was centered around what was best for you. What would keep you most comfortable. Even if that meant your life would be shortened.*

You earned the attention of the man running for President, you became his poster child for the need for a National Patients' Bill of Rights. You went to the 2000 Democratic Presidential Convention in Los Angeles. That man checked in on your progress and care for all your days and sent a loving tribute when you left us.

You died on a Saturday morning. It was 5am and the cat that slept with you every night came upstairs and woke me up. By doing so, I was able to be with you as you left this earth - it was a debt that I could never repay to that cat. I felt your spirit pass through me and I knew you were at peace. I cried tears of happiness for you and grief and sorrow for me.

Your life was one that touched many. You inspired so many people to do and be things they may not have done if not for you. And Ian? I am at the top of that list. I was lost and not sure what I wanted to be when I grew up when you entered my life. You gave me focus. You gave me purpose. You showed me what life was all about.

Here we are, fifteen years after your birth. While you will always be a four-year-old little boy in my mind's eye.... I like to think you are free, that your body doesn't dictate what you can and cannot do. I picture you smiling, talking, singing, enjoying foods....

Ian - I hope you are okay with the decisions I made for you. I would have died in your place, were that possible. I like to think that someday - I will be able to face you and tell you just how much I love you. How much you have meant and mean to me. The positive impact you have had on my life. I want to see you smile and hear you tell me it's all okay.

Happy birthday, my Zoopie. Thank you for all you have given to me and others. You will live in my heart for all my days, and I will always think of you with a smile on my face and warmth in my heart. I have no idea what it would be like to have you here with me in this life now... but, really, I guess I do. For you will always be a part of me.

It is no secret that trauma and tragedy change a person. I don't know who I would be if not for the things I've been through. I don't spend time feeling sorry for myself. I can't stand the word "fair," especially when I hear someone talk about life not being fair. It isn't fair nor is it equitable. Some people live their entire lives without trauma or tragedy.

I've often said that I'm grateful for the experiences I've been through because they've made me the person I am and I'm happy with who I am. Truthfully, that is complete crap. I wouldn't wish my horrible experiences on anyone. I can, however, say that I understand empathy more than most people. I can talk to a person who has undergone the worst thing in their life, and I do so with compassion and an understanding of what it takes to survive. There is no conversation I shy away from.

One of the questions I'm often asked by people who've survived an awful experience is "When will I feel like I did before this happened?" The answer is, "You never will." You can't erase what happened, how you felt when it happened, or how you feel in the aftermath. This is the first truth a person must accept.

Not getting back to how you felt before isn't all bad. I have my memories of Vince, John, and Ian. Good memories. And, after a time, those good memories are what takes the largest space in my mind when I think of each of them.

I can relate to people who've had an awful childhood, people who've survived things they really don't want to talk about or even remember. I can relate to people who've survived the loss of a loved one… via a sudden accident as well as unexpected suicide. Lastly, I can relate to people who've lost a child. Not only can I relate, but I am also comfortable and willing to talk about what happened and how they feel. I know, more than most people, that there aren't any "right" words to say to someone who has experienced an awful event. Sometimes, just listening – even if the person isn't talking – is the best thing you can do.

I've learned that life is short, and people can die at any age. I've learned that mental illness is something we all need to talk about, and the stigma of suicide needs to be addressed. I've learned that we aren't promised anything in this life and to be happy with what I have. I've learned how to love another person fully and completely, even though I know the grief of what it feels like to lose someone I care for so deeply.

One of the most important things I have learned is that I will never get an apology from the providers that caused my son's death. I've forgiven them, for to keep anger inside of me only harms me.

> *"Life sometimes becomes easier when you learn to accept the apology you never got."*
>
> *– Robert Brault*

Chapter 22:

Life Changes

"There are things that we don't want to happen but have to accept, things we don't want to know but have to learn, and people we can't live without but have to let go."

– Unknown

In the classes I teach about grieving, I advise people to not make any major changes within the first year once they experience a great loss. This is exceptionally good advice, though I've not always followed it myself.

After Vince died, I packed up everything I owned and moved across the country to forget him. His memories followed me.

After John died, I packed up all his things and donated them to charity. I moved to a new house and purged nearly everything I had that reminded me of him. His memories followed me.

After Ian died, I thought I'd learned about grief, so I stayed in the same house, and kept so many of his items. Thirteen years after his death – I thought it was time to close that chapter on my life and move. His memories followed me.

I've come to realize that I cannot escape the memories. I cannot try to keep only the good memories. I must keep them all. They are all a part of who I am. To deny the painful memories is to deny part of the person I miss. None of us is perfect, we all come with good and bad intentions. To fully appreciate the good memories, I must acknowledge the bad ones. That's part of life.

In 2017, 13 years after Ian died, I felt that I was ready to move from my home of 20+ years. I went through closets and boxes that hadn't been touched in years. I called it the "Great Purge" as I made numerous trips to the thrift store with donations, as well as to the dump. Packing up the memories I had of Ian was hard. I read through old newspaper articles about my family, and I stroked one of the quilts I'd kept. I was filled with doubt – "Is this really what I want to do?" Then, one day, I found a letter on my front porch. It was from a couple who wrote that they were interested in buying my house. The house was not on the market yet, so they had no idea I was planning to move. As I read the note, I found out that the wife was a NICU nurse. Then, I found out the husband was a childhood friend of one of my neighbors. It seemed meant to be. I sent the couple an email and I told them my story. I told them about Ian, that he lived and died in that home. I told them about the Golden Chain tree in the backyard and expressed the importance that they leave it there forever. When I met that couple in person, I had a sense that they were perfect for that house.

Chapter 23:

The End Was Inevitable

"Celebrate endings – for they precede new beginnings."

– Jonathan Lockwood Huiel

I could cite several research studies on the marriages that don't survive the loss of a child. In the days after Ian's death, I remember Dylan and I doing our own things. I began to work nonstop, sometimes 80+ hours a week. I would fill my days with those things that I could control. I was professional and I was known as "the Ice Queen." I did not delve into anything emotional and, as I look back, I am sorry for my lack of presence with my children.

I was unhappy. I remember thinking, after Ian died, the providers responsible for Ian's injuries and death took something very important away from me. Anything else I lost, would be me giving it to them. That included my marriage. Though I was unhappy, to admit my marriage was failing was to give those providers one more thing. I refused to do that. So... I stayed in an unhappy marriage for many years.

I took a new job at a local healthcare organization. I loved my work, and I loved my co-workers. I loved my boss, a woman named Jude. She became a mentor to me. Jude was a strong, powerful woman. She helped me understand how to deal with situations that were uncomfortable for me, such as an emotional employee. Before working with Jude, I was incredibly uncomfortable with an employee showing any emotion. Jude taught me the technique of sliding a box of tissues across the table and saying, "I can see that you are upset."

Those simple words helped me become a better leader. I dedicated my Medical Office Management textbook to Jude.

As the years after Ian's death went by, I became increasingly unhappy. Dylan left his job after Ian died. This left me as the sole provider for our family and I resented that. Dylan eventually finished college and found a job. Once he was able to support himself, I saw my way out. I told him I wanted a divorce. He wasn't thrilled with the idea, and it took some time to get him to move out. We each hired an attorney and I tried to make things as amicable as possible. Money was a thing – Dylan couldn't access any of our joint assets until we had a divorce agreement. He rented a home not far from mine and I agreed to him taking furnishings from our home. I bought supplies for him, such as dishes, beddings, towels, etc. Still, he felt like he was shorted. Dylan was adamant that our children should enjoy the same material items at his house as they did at mine, though he could not afford that lifestyle on his own income. I felt guilty, so I accommodated his requests for material things.

The end finally came in 2013. We agreed to a divorce settlement. Dylan bought a house nearby and we agreed to a 50/50 shared custody. We continued to use the same babysitter we'd had for several years – she picked the kids up from school and supervised them at the home of the parent who had custody that day. This worked for a while and shared custody had its benefits. The kids got two birthdays, and two Christmas celebrations each year.

A couple of years after our divorce, Dylan remarried. Shortly thereafter, Dylan convinced his wife that they should move to Florida. Dylan had always been a major fan of Disney and wanted to be close to the Disney parks. His wife agreed and they moved to Florida. Dylan filed a parenting plan revision.

My son Riley was 10 years old at the time and I engaged my attorney to discuss solutions. My options were to fight for full custody, or to agree to a shared custodial agreement. At that time, Dylan and his wife had two more children. Dylan's wife had family in the Seattle area, including parents and siblings that were involved in the kids' lives. My son had never experienced the grandparent relationship and now his dad was moving him thousands of miles away from the new grandparents he had.

Riley was the oldest of the children at his dad's house, and he was fond of and close to those siblings. I wanted to keep Riley with me full time, but I realized those siblings were an important part of Riley's life. I put what I wanted aside and went with what I thought was best for my son. I agreed that Riley would spend the school year in Florida and fly home to Seattle for long weekends and all vacation breaks. That decision was hard for me. I knew I had an excellent case for fighting for full custody... but my mom heart wanted to do what was best for my son, not what was best for me. That decision has weighed heavy on my heart over the years. As each year passes, I try to support my son and let him know I love him and want the best for him.

Chapter 24:

Lessons Learned

"The best and most beautiful things in the world cannot be seen nor even touched, but just felt in the heart."

– Helen Keller

During his short life, Ian delighted in simple things. He liked to be spun around in his wheelchair. His giggle was a delight to hear. For whatever reason, Ian responded to yellow. We had stuffed toys that were yellow, and I made blankets for him with yellow fabric. When he saw something yellow, Ian's eyes would grow wide, and he would smile and giggle.

One of my lessons from Ian included slowing down. Slowing down for something as simple as enjoying the color yellow.

On days when I am feeling down, days when I am sad, frustrated, or just generally letting life get the best of me... Ian visits in the form of the color yellow. Sometimes it is yellow flowers that I see blooming in a yard on my daily walks. Sometimes it is a yellow car parked next to mine. Sometimes it is hearing the song *Yellow* by the band Coldplay. I always know when my Ian is near when yellow is around.

About 15 years after Ian died, I felt it was time for me to give away his wheelchair. I contacted a local company that finds homes for used medical equipment and was put in contact with a woman who lived near me. The woman had twin foster children, both of whom were severely disabled and in need of a wheelchair. Ian's chair helped not one, but two children.

We all write our own story, it's our narrative. We take our life experiences, and we adapt. The challenge is to adapt in a positive way.

I visit Ian's grave frequently. For the first year after he died, I visited daily. At some point, I found myself visiting only one or two times per week. I know each of us finds solace in different ways as we grieve. For me, having a grave to visit brings me peace. Placing flowers and stuffed animals on Ian's grave makes me feel closer to him. Dylan designed Ian's headstone. There is an etched drawing of Ian in his wheelchair, some shamrocks to celebrate his Irish DNA, a porcelain photograph of Ian's smiling face, and the phrase, "Your memory is the light that guides us."

As a child, I dreamed of being in a happy place. I didn't expect that a happy place doesn't exist. Happiness is a direction, not a place. Happiness can be fleeting and none of us is owed a happy life. Some of us learn through trauma and tragedy the value of happiness in just one moment in time.

I am who I am because of my life experiences. Though I wouldn't wish some of those experiences on even my worst enemy, I am happy with who I am. I am happy with the contribution I give to others, especially my students. I can say that my life has taught me that nothing may be taken for granted. If I want to be happy, if I want to be content, if I want to be a functioning member of society – I have only myself to rely on to make those things happen. It's work. Sometimes hard work.

In 2019, I married my third husband. Ours was an outdoor wedding and included friends and close family. I chose a copper-colored dress that I found on eBay for $80. All my children were part of the wedding ceremony – my two daughters were bridesmaids and my two sons walked me down the aisle. Wait – my THREE sons were there. I'd commissioned an angel pin to wear to signify Ian was with me as well.

My wedding in July, 2019

Over the years, I've had several people who hear parts of my story say things like, "I don't know how you've survived that," or, "You must be the strongest person I know." I don't always answer those statements with words but, in my head, I'm thinking, "What are the alternatives?" We don't always get to choose what is thrown at us in life. And we can't always predict who and what we will become.

For example, I didn't expect that I would one day become the Spider Killer.

> *"One day, you will tell your story of how you overcame what you went through, and it will be someone else's survival guide."*
>
> *–Brene Brown*

CPSIA information can be obtained
at www.ICGtesting.com
Printed in the USA
LVHW020931170423
744535LV00010BA/618